TRAVELING BY TIN LIZZIE

TRAVELING BY TIN LIZZIE

The Great Model-T Road Trip of 1924

Laura Purtymun McBride

Original ©1980 Laura Purtymun McBride
Copyright assigned 1994
to Sedona Historical Society.
All rights reserved.

Republished 2008 by James W. Eaton
for the Sedona Historical Society.

© 2008 by Sedona Historical Society

Cover painting by Karen Denison.

ISBN: 978-0615570273

Printed in the United States of America

Published by Sedona Heritage Publishing

The Sedona Historical Society
operates the Sedona Heritage Museum;
PO Box 10216, Sedona, AZ 86339

www.sedonamuseum.org

Originally dedicated by Laura Purtymun McBride:
"To the memory of my father and my mother,
Albert W. Purtymun and Clara Thompson Purtymun."

And dedicated 2008 by the members of the
Sedona Historical Society
to the memory of our Co-Founder, second President,
Historian and good friend, Laura Purtymun McBride.

Acknowledgements

By the Author:

The stories that were written in this book are from the viewpoint of a thirteen-year-old girl who went on a trip and many years later wrote this account.

Other members of the family may have altogether different opinions of each incident.

I want to thank the many people who have helped in putting this book together — especially Dorothy Murphy and my co-workers in the writing class I attended in Sedona. I also wish to thank Gladys Ticer and Gwendolyn Towne for their many hours of typing.

Laura Purtymun McBride

By the Publisher:

We thank Laura's daughter, Gwendolyn Towne, and her niece, Kay Knight, without whose valuable help the republication of this book would not have been possible.

For the Sedona Historical Society,
Jim Eaton

Foreword

This is Laura's book as she wrote it, scanned from the original camera-ready plates. Nothing has been changed except for the addition of this foreword. Please remember that references to "the present" or "now" mean the time the book was written, before 1980.

A very few of the original photos were replaced by similar ones taken near the same time. Most in this book are from Sedona Historical Society archives or from original prints loaned by Kay Knight. The rest had to be scanned from a copy of the original book.

Laura Purtymun was born Nov. 9, 1910 at Crescent Moon Ranch near what is now called Red Rock Crossing. Her parents were Albert Purtymun and Clara Ellen Thompson Purtymun. Her mother's parents were James J. Thompson, the first white settler in the Sedona area, and Maggie James Thompson. Maggie's parents were Abraham and Elizabeth James, the area's first homesteaders. Laura's paternal grandparents were Stephen and Martha Purtymun. Martha Purtymun's father was the legendary "Bear" Howard.

Laura was "The First Lady of the Sedona Historical Society". She was a co-founder, the first Historian, and 1987 President of the Society. She was also the oldest continuous resident of the Sedona area, and made many important contributions to the preservation and teaching of the area's heritage.

Laura had a legendary sense of humor, and it was a delight to attend a Society meeting with her. She enjoyed spinning tales of early Sedona, and was featured speaker before numerous groups as well as on radio and TV

(continued on page viii)

(continued from page vii)

shows. In addition to this book, she wrote many stories and newspaper columns.

At a time when few women worked on construction jobs, Laura used unique materials in building walls at her Oak Creek Canyon home. Creek bed stones, shells, broken china, old bottles, and all kinds of durable curios are creatively embedded in the walls, which remain a monument to her energy and lively imagination.

But beyond all that, Laura was modest and had a self-deprecating humor. Here's a sample of how she described herself:

"Maybe it was (my parents') longing for a boy that caused the stork to pick out such a large bundle. He perched in the top of the big cottonwood tree over our tent to get his bearings. The weight of the blanket caused the knot to slip out of his mouth and I came tumbling down.

"Time did nothing to improve my frame. As a child and young girl, my dresses always hung on my body like a sheet wrapped around a ghost. At a time when exposing a knee was a disgrace, mine were always exposed. To get a dress long enough, I had to get one big enough to wrap around twice."

On Aug. 4, 1932 Laura married William Ray McBride, who was working in the Clemenceau smelter. They had two children, Gwendolyn and Ted. Ray died in 1979.

Laura passed away on July 1, 1994. Her good humor and sharp wit live on in the memories of those lucky enough to have known her.

James W. Eaton

CONTENTS

1. Getting Ready 1
2. Caravan Underway 8
3. Mormon Lake 12
4. Mamma and Papa Take Leave....................................... 19
5. Wedding Day and an Unfortunate Occurrence............22
6. Changing Tires... 29
7. Albuquerque Campground.. 33
8. The Rocky Mountain Trail... 37
9. Parachute Creek and Narrow Escapes......................... 44
10. Adventures in Salt Lake City 50
11. Unwelcome in Wagner 61
12., Stalking a Cornfield 65
13. Home in a Potato Cellar 68
14. The Great Flood 73
15. Prune-Pickers in the Orchard...................................... 78
16. Water 82
17. Columbia River Country 89
18. Among the Apple Farmers 95
19. Stocking Caps and Streetcar Tracks......................... 105
20. Oregon Passage 109
21. Wintering in Cottonwood... 115
22. Christmas..123
23. Yard-Camped at Grandma Cook's............................... 128
24 Brand New Shoes...133
25. Grandpa Purtymun's Old Store................................... 139
26. Oil Strips 'Cross the Desert...................................... 144
27. The Sky Is Falling.. 149
28. No Brakes on Mingus Mountain................................. 155
29. Tea and Sandwiches... 170
30. What Happened After...176

CHAPTER ONE

Getting Ready

The biggest event in my life at the age of eleven was leaving Sedona and moving to Clemenceau. Sedona in the early twenties was just a few farms scattered along the creek. There were no public buildings except the ranger station and the one-room schoolhouse where the first eight grades of school were taught. The post office at that time was up in Oak Creek Canyon at the Thompson ranch, my grandparents' home. In our houses there was no indoor plumbing, and our only fuel was wood. The water supply was Oak Creek. The water was either dipped out of a ditch or hauled in a barrel that stood by the kitchen door. We had no electricity; our homes were lit with coal-oil lamps, and for outside lighting we used coal-oil lanterns.

Clemenceau, twenty-five miles west of Sedona, was the company town for the United Verde Extension Mining Company, owners of the Clemenceau smelter. Papa had obtained a job in the smelter so my older sisters could go to high school in Clarkdale, another smelter town.

We had to live in two houses in Clemenceau because the available ones had but two rooms, a kitchen and combination living and bedroom. Our size family just couldn't squeeze into one house. We lived here only a short time before Papa bought a house in Smelter City, a suburb of Cottonwood.

This was real city living for us Sedonians. The big town of Cottonwood had a grocery, a drygoods, a drugstore, and even a silent motion picture show. The schoolhouse I went to there was so big there were only two grades in my room.

Almost two years had passed and we were still living in the same house in Smelter City, when my family came up with the big idea of taking the trip. I don't know what inspired them to try something so wonderful. Mamma said Papa wanted to see his Dad, whom he hadn't seen in years. Although Grandpa Purtymun lived in California, and the border between Arizona and California was closed with a quarantine because of a hoof-and-mouth disease that was raging among cattle in Old Mexico, it did seem a little strange when our plans were made to travel east through New Mexico and over most of the western states in order to reach California.

I think the reason we made this trip in such a round about way was because the adventurous spirit of both my parents was looking for an outlet. It seemed to have been part of the makeup on either side of our ancestry.

My mother's dad ran away from home in Londonderry, Ireland when he was just a kid in his early teens. He'd caught a ship to New York and then with another boy his age, had gone on to Galveston, Texas hoping they could fight Indians. My Dad's folks had crossed the great California desert in a covered wagon when the Indians were still on the rampage.

Since I could remember, my parents always seemed to be looking for greener pastures somewhere. We never stayed in one place long. We were always moving from

Albert and Clara Purtymun with their first baby, Della, around 1904.

house to house in Sedona or up in the Canyon. One time we even moved to Phoenix for three months. Now we were actually going to leave Arizona. I had never even dreamed of going so far away.

I, Laura Purtymun, happened to be that freckle-faced, gawky eleven-year-old who was so excited about moving from Sedona. It would have been impossible to say how lucky I felt when I heard about this big trip to Oregon and back home through California. Someone had told Papa

Laura Purtymun (right) just before the move from Sedona to Clemenceau, wading in the irrigation ditch with Violet and Bud.

there was a lot of money to be made working in the big apple orchards along the Columbia River. We hoped to reach there by fall and get rich before continuing our travels.

My Papa, Albert Purtymun, had been considered tall as a young man, but through the years hard work and back trouble had caused him to stoop. His unruly brown hair, now streaked with gray, was parted on the left side and combed back over a high forehead. Beneath heavy brows his honest gray eyes looked out on a world he trusted. He was an easygoing fellow, who left most important decisions to his wife, Clara. He had all he could handle keeping food in our mouths and a roof over our heads. At thirty-five, Mamma was a nice-looking woman. She was six years younger than Papa. Mamma spoke in a low voice, but we could always tell by the tone when we had better obey. I never remember a spanking from either of them.

Somehow they had managed to save one hundred dollars to start this trip. With only five kids left to feed, they thought that ample money to grubstake us for awhile.

Della, my oldest sister, always neat and clean herself, worked hard trying to make me look like a lady. She was always after me to comb my hair and wash my face. She was talented too; she could make her own clothes, crochet, knit, embroider and even tat. Della had quit school and was working away from home. She had celebrated her twentieth birthday in May and was engaged to a nice young man. They planned on getting married and going with us on this trip. With no big boys in our family, we all liked having Kenneth Greenwell added to our tribe.

Erma, my second sister, was a sweet dark-haired little beauty. Her husband, Walter Baker, was a tall, slender ex-cowboy. He was older than Kenneth and more quiet. Walter was dark; Kenneth had a sandy complexion and was much shorter than Walter. Walter had a soft voice, a big smile he used often, and he moved slowly. Kenneth didn't bother to smile; when he was ready to laugh, he just opened his mouth and let the laughter roll out. Whenever Kenneth had anything that needed doing, he didn't believe in fooling around. If it needed doing he dug right into it. We had known Walter back in Sedona when the round-up camped there on their way to and

Walter Baker in 1912, age sixteen, riding a horse he tamed.

Getting Ready

from the mountain each spring and fall. We were all glad when Erma and Walter asked to go with us. Now we would have six grown-ups, five kids and Erma's medium-sized brown dog to start our trip.

The week before we left seemed endless to me. Everyone was busy packing and making last minute arrangements. Our belongings were packed in cement sacks and dynamite boxes. Papa had made lids for the boxes out of scrap lumber and the hinges were of strips of old shoe leather. I would have enjoyed helping, but no, I had to entertain my little sister and brothers and get them out of everyone's way. I couldn't even pick out what I wanted to take without being told, "There isn't room for that junk."

I couldn't see why I couldn't take what I wanted. Virgie, not much older than I, was allowed a box of her own. Virgie thought, just because she was a bookworm and had skipped a grade in school, she was something special. After her sixteenth birthday in April she wouldn't even play with me, just hung around the grown-ups. Anyway, Violet, my younger sister, was almost eight. She could take care of baby Chuckles. Why did I have to watch Bud, our oldest brother? He'd be old enough to go to school next fall.

CHAPTER TWO

Caravan Underway

Our caravan of three Model-Ts got underway at ten o'clock in the morning on June 6, 1924. We weren't actually starting on the trip yet, we were only moving out of our house so we could rent it. We had to wait until our renter received his first paycheck from his work at the smelter before he could pay the rent. We were only going up on the mountain where it was cooler to wait and do some last-minute work on our car. Mamma and Papa would go back down to Smelter City later and collect the money so we could really get started.

Our truck was the first to pull out. Mamma, holding Chuckles, had arranged herself on the seat beside Papa. In the back of the truck where the mattresses were placed on top of the other stuff, we kids were perched. Next in line were Erma and Walter in their lovely little roadster with a windshield and canvas top. Behind the cab on a small platform was stacked their bedding and all their worldly possessions.

Kenneth's strip-down (a Model-T with no fenders or

bed, only a seat) brought up the rear. He had built a platform behind the seat big enough for a bed. Here is where he and Della would sleep after they were married in Flagstaff. I guess he thought the ground wasn't good enough for his bride on her honeymoon.

Kenneth was going as far as Stoneman Lake with us to help Papa and Walter build a canvas top and a windshield for our big family limousine. He would then return to the valley to bring Della up to join us. She had promised her boss one last week of work before leaving.

It was eleven when we arrived at Montezuma's Well. Papa figured we had better pull over and eat lunch, as that was the last water hole for the cars and the kids until we reached Stoneman Lake.

I was feeling a little puny before we stopped for lunch, and by the time the food was ready I felt more like vomiting than eating. This was very disturbing to Mamma. I was never too sick to eat, even when we had the flu and measles. Of all her seven children, I was noted for having the biggest mouth and a stomach that always seemed to be empty. After discussing all the symptoms of known diseases, my parents thought it best to spend the night at Montezuma's Well. Maybe a good night's sleep, after all the excitement of the past week, would bring me back to normal.

In the morning I was feeling somewhat better, so we started up the mountain. As the terrain grew steeper and rougher, we came to deep cuts that had been made by the road builders through the blue volcanic formations. That was why this road was called the Blue Grade. We were probably halfway up the winding curves of the Blue Grade before I became so miserable my mouth flew open and the real sounds of agony started coming out. Papa drove the twenty-five miles to the lake in low gear in order to hit the potholes and rocks as gently as possible. He thought that might ease my pains.

I heard later that I missed a lot of wonderful sights,

Younger members of the Purtymun clan, around 1922. Left to right, Virgie, Della, Erma, Chuckles, Bud, Violet and Laura.

but at the time I could think of nothing but my misery. I doubt if anyone else thought much about the scenery either. The sound of my bawling was so loud it could be heard above the chug of the motor and the rattle of our old Tin Lizzies.

Upon reaching the lake, Kenneth and Walter headed back down the rough road on the rescue mission to the nearest doctor. In Camp Verde, a distance of thirty miles, they found an old country doctor. He diagnosed my ailment as food poisoning. The pills they brought back did the trick and in a short time I was my normal self.

Our menfolks then went to work on our car. It looked pretty when they had completed the new top and windshield, with the material we had brought along with us. Now we wouldn't have to worry about the hot sun and rain.

At the end of the week Kenneth went back to get Della. She brought the package of traveling clothes Mamma had asked her to pick up. I don't remember what the

Caravan Underway 11

other kids got. Mine were some romper-type, drop-seat coveralls. They had little pockets sticking out on each side and were trimmed in red, my favorite color. They would have looked lovely on a delicate little lady, but when I put them on, the ankle-length legs were about three inches above my shoes. I had to wear these all during the trip and they kept shrinking or my legs kept growing, until they became knee pants.

CHAPTER THREE

Mormon Lake

From the time I can first remember, lunch always took place in our home before twelve noon. At eleven sharp, on the way to Lake Mary, our next destination, we pulled out into a little meadow surrounded by pines and pinon trees, although the other two flivvers weren't in sight yet. When we left Stoneman Lake my older sisters were milling around the campfire, combing their hair and powdering their faces, so Papa figured they would pull in by the time lunch was ready. They weren't too good at cooking in the Dutch oven anyway.

Violet, always trying to do whatever I did, and five-year-old Bud had followed me up on the hillside where I was searching for pinon gum. I had just found a likely tree when Mamma started calling, "Laura! Come down here and take care of this baby if you want any dinner."

It wasn't enough that I was letting Violet and Bud tag along behind me; now I had to add Chuckles to my collection.

As I neared camp I heard Papa grumbling, "This will be hellish-looking bacon when I get through mangling it with this axe."

Mamma, about half laughing, said, "If you can't slice bacon with an axe, how do you think I'm going to peel potatoes? I guess we'll just have biscuits and gravy." It was then that I found that the box containing all the silver was in Kenneth's car.

When Walter, Erma and Virgie drove in a little later and Papa asked what had happened to Kenneth, Walter said, "They were ready to leave when we left the lake, but we haven't seen a sign of them since we pulled away from the camp."

Walter happened to have a pocket knife, so Papa whittled some spoons out of a piece of wood for us to scoop our bread and gravy into our mouths. We had just finished eating all the bacon and gravy when Della and Kenneth appeared on the scene. Kenneth had a big smear of grease on his face. His clothes and hands gave him the appearance of a mechanic who had just completed an eight-hour shift in a busy garage.

"I'm hungry as a dog! What've, you got to eat?" Kenneth growled as he crawled from his strip-down.

Virgie, getting her two-bits' worth in, retorted, "It's too late now. If you hadn't spent so much time spooning you'd of been here in time."

"Spooning HELL!" Kenneth said, "Look at my hands!" He grabbed a biscuit and a raw potato and started gnawing ravenously. "We've only had thirteen flat tires since we left Stoneman Lake." Della, being a lady and not having done any of the tire work, was satisfied with biscuits and preserves.

Between bites Kenneth lamented, "I'm going to have to do something about my tire situation before we leave

Flag." He had already traded two of his worn tires to his brother Carl for new ones. Now he was going to have to do something about the other two.

When we reloaded the car after lunch, Papa made sure we added the silverware box to our load. I didn't blame him; it looked like quite a job whittling out all those spoons, and I prefer having my gravy on potatoes instead of on old cold biscuits.

By mid-afternoon we drove out of the pine forest to be confronted with the biggest body of water I had ever seen. I wondered, as I watched the waves tumbling over each other, could this be what the ocean looked like?

Papa called over his shoulder to us kids in the truck-bed, "This is Mormon Lake, named after a group of Mormons that had a dairy here years ago."

Previously, around the campfire at Stoneman Lake, Papa had told us how in nineteen hundred and two, he had driven through the middle of Mormon Lake. At that time he had been swamping (odd-job boy) for a freight outfit that traveled between Flagstaff and Payson. In later years the local cattlemen had used the meadow, where the lake now stands, as a sort of rodeo ground. They practiced roping, did their branding, and broke their horses to ride there. Papa said when the drought broke and the mountain was covered with snow for the next fifteen years, the meadow turned into a lake.

We wandered in and out of coves, on the west side of the lake, for the next seven miles. Papa told us that in places the lake was fourteen feet deep and three miles across.

Leaving Mormon Lake, we found ourselves in the tall timber for another fourteen miles before we came to Lake Mary, a man-made lake. It looked small after seeing Mormon Lake.

Not to be outdone by Papa, Mamma told of the time soon after they were married when Papa brought her and

Mormon Lake

some friends over to this area. There were a lot of caverns in the volcanic formation. They built a fire and with burning pitch knots for light they explored the caverns and found many with solid ice floors. After the dam was built to collect the water for the lake, the caverns were filled with water.

We reached the campground at the north end of the lake, just as the sun was disappearing behind the pines. Papa glanced up at the setting sun and said, "We'd better get a move-on if we're going to get supper over and the beds made before dark."

Mamma immediately began dishing out chores. As usual I got my share. "Laura, take the kids and drag up some wood. Virgie, you start making beds as soon's the men get the mattresses off the truck."

Papa and Walter had unloaded three mattresses, bedding, numerous boxes, Dutch ovens, and other paraphernalia onto the ground; then Walter joined Erma, who was trying to unload their car. The mound behind the cab looked like one of the San Francisco Peaks. It was stacked as high as the car roof. The only place left for their dog Brownie to ride was in the fender well, a space on the running board built to carry a tire.

Suddenly Mamma let out a yell. "Laura, get the kids behind a tree! Here comes Kenneth!" Della and Kenneth had been detailed to pick up some groceries at the Lake Mary store before coming on to camp.

Kenneth always had trouble finding the perfect place to park his vehicle for his night's lodging. It's a wonder he hadn't run over one of us. He probably would have, if Mamma hadn't been so alert and always warned us of his coming. He would whiz that strip-down first one way then another in his search for a level spot. He wanted to park away from us noisy kids' bed, away from the smoke of our campfire and where the sun wouldn't shine in his eyes in the morning.

Papa, who was breaking wood for the campfire, could

be heard muttering, "Damn fool kid! Won't he ever grow up?"

Mamma always had a horror of finding a hair in her food. She never allowed us to comb our hair near her cooking. Human hair was one thing, but when it came to a dog's or a cat's hair, well, there just couldn't be anything dirtier. Our dogs and cats were never allowed in the house, period. If a dog or cat rubbed against her clothes she would change them immediately. If a dog licked her hand, soap and water would hardly remove the germs. To keep Mamma happy we all worked together to protect her from this filth. Now she was having trouble with Erma's hound. "Erma, come get this crazy dog. He'll have hairs in the biscuits and everything." Mamma's hands were covered with flour and dough. She was doing her best to push Brownie away with her foot. "Get away! Go on!" she almost screamed.

Erma, with a can of corn she had opened in one hand and an iron skillet in the other, began calling, "Brownie, Brownie! "

Papa came to the rescue with a biscuit he had dug out of the bread can. "Come here, Brownie," he coaxed. "Leave Mom alone. Take this and go over by Erma's bed. That's a good dog." Brownie grabbed the biscuit in his mouth and trotted off to lie down.

With the dog out of the way, Mamma went back to her biscuit making. "Dad, you'd better get the Dutch oven off the fire; these biscuits are ready to cook," she said. Papa immediately began looking for the gancho. It seemed to always be missing when someone wanted it and we kids would always get the blame.

Our gancho was made from a green limb approximately two feet long and two inches around. All the branches were cut off the limb except one on the large end; this branch was cut off about two inches from the main limb forming a hook. When cooking with a Dutch oven, a shovel to handle the coals and a gancho to move the oven and lid are absolute necessities.

Sure enough, this time Bud had taken the gancho to use the hook to pull his old shoe box filled with rocks up a make-believe hill. It's funny. One kid does something wrong, and we all get the blame.

With supper over and the dishes washed, more wood was put on the fire to ward off the night's chill. We kids

Papa uses a Dutch oven to cook quail on a Thanksgiving picnic near Humboldt, Arizona, around 1930.

were lying on our bed playing "Everybody Ready," the only quiet game we knew. The grown-ups were sitting around the fire discussing the day's happenings. All at once the night air vibrated with a terrible scream. Everyone jumped to their feet. The little kids started crying and shoved me away from Mamma where I had taken refuge. There was a second scream before Papa could grab the shovel -- the only weapon handy -- and pushing us kids out of his way, he ran in the direction of the noise. When he got away from the light of the fire, he could see Erma standing as though she was petrified in the bright moonlight. She yelled, "Snake!" and pointed to what looked like a clump of grass. Papa brought the shovel down with a clop. By now everyone had gathered around and could see it was a rattlesnake. In a voice still trembling with fear, Erma explained, "I saw a big pitch knot over here before dark. I was searching for it so I could put it on the fire. I touched what I thought was a clump of grass with this stick in my hand, and the darned thing rattled. I was so surprised I couldn't move."

That was one night I didn't argue with Virgie about sleeping on the outside. I crawled into the blankets close to Mamma's bed and refused to move.

CHAPTER FOUR

Mamma and Papa Take Leave

    I was awakened by the sound of breaking wood; and peeking out from under the blankets I could see someone building the fire in the cold, shadowy dawn. I wondered why anybody would be getting up this early. Then I remembered, Mamma and Papa were going back to Smelter City to pick up our rent money, and this was also the day Della had picked to get married. I thought, "Why the rush?" and I pulled the covers back over my head. I hoped no one would bother me until the sun came up.
    The next thing I knew, Chuckles was pulling the bedding off me as he whimpered, "Mamma told you to dress me." I could hear Mamma beating something. It sounded like it could be hotcake batter. The thought of Mamma's hotcakes floating in homemade sugar syrup

was more than I could resist. Hurrying into my duds, and poking Chuckles into his, I made it to the chow line before most of the gang. I hadn't bothered to wash.

Mamma spotted me getting my graniteware plate. "Have you washed?" she questioned me. When I came back from my quick dip everyone but Papa was ahead of me.

Mamma always said Papa was late for everything because he was always puttering. Now she called, "Dad, get over here and eat. You're making a lot of dust flopping that canvas around. If we plan on getting back up here tonight we're going to have to hurry. Kenneth and Walter can put that fly up after we leave." Papa headed for the wash pan after attaching one last piece of bailing wire to the corner of the canvas.

This fly was the only protection we had from the elements for many months. It was only a small canvas stretched over a ridgepole with each corner staked to the ground with wire. It wasn't much, but it did protect our food from the hot sun or a light rain.

After breakfast the little kids wandered over to a junk pile left by former campers. While they were rummaging through the garbage they found some interesting cans and bottles and they decided to play house and have Chuckles for their baby. They would play like their baby had wet his pants and needed changing. Violet pulled Chuckles' pants down and Bud poured what they thought was baby oil on his little butt, just like they had seen Mamma do so many times. Chuckles' reaction surprised them: he started crying and ran toward camp. His screams caused Mamma to rush to meet him. The only information she could get out of Chuckles was *"Hurt!"* and more crying as he dug at his seat. The mystery was solved when Mamma saw Violet and Bud hiding behind an old stump. They told her what they had done and showed her the bottle they had used. It was only rubbing alcohol. Mamma washed Chuckles and put clean clothes on him and once more he was our smiling baby. After putting Chuckles in the pickup seat Mamma climbed in beside him to wait for Papa to crank their means of transportation. Papa already had one hind wheel jacked up. Jacking up one hind wheel and releasing the emergency brake put the car in high gear, which made the motor turn over easier and start better. On cold nights the radiator was drained to keep it from freezing, then filled with boiling water in the morning. This helped to warm the motor. Even after all this work, sometimes it would take two men taking turns at the crank a half an hour to get a car started.

You would think Mamma would have known better than to get in our car before she heard the motor running. She was getting very impatient as Papa cranked for awhile, then Walter would try for a round. This had been going on for some time when Kenneth, returning from his morning nature call, arrived and took his turn. One quick spin and the motor sputted then took off in its usual way.

"Well, I'll be doggoned," Papa said, "We should've waited for you instead of using up all our energy."

"Yeh, that's what we'll do next time," Walter agreed.

"I think you two stopped one second too soon. The car was waiting for one more spin before it would start. I happened along at just the right time," Kenneth answered.

Papa ambled around and climbed in under the steering wheel. He pulled the emergency brake on. This took the car out of gear and the jacked-up wheel quit turning. Kenneth removed the jack, and now with all four wheels on the ground and the motor running, Mamma and Papa were at last on their way. As they drove off, Mamma's voice, giving last minute instructions, was still ringing in our ears.

CHAPTER FIVE

Wedding Day and an Unfortunate Occurrence

This was the sixth of June, the day Della and Kenneth had picked for their wedding day. Della put on her wedding gown of white Spanish lace trimmed with pink and blue ribbons. She had made it herself and had spent days working on it. It must've cost her a gob of money. It was worth all the money and time, though, because she looked just like a princess. I thought she must be the most beautiful bride that ever existed.

Even though I put on my most dejected air and forced a tear or two, they drove off to their Justice of the Peace wedding without me. Erma and Walter took them in their little coupe. There wasn't even room for Virgie; she usually managed to get in on anything important. This time she had to stay and be in charge of camp and us kids. We sure needed her; all she did was sit and read.

Leaving the Justice of the Peace's office, the wedding party went out to the Flagstaff dump to look for tires for Kenneth's car. They were in luck; they found several good ones some rich idiot had thrown away.

The shadows of the pines had grown long, pushing the sunny areas ahead of them out of our campground. The supper file had burned down to glowing coals that seemed to be waiting for the Dutch ovens. Walter and

Wedding Day and an Unfortunate Occurrence

Kenneth were rustling wood for the fire and the girls were preparing supper, when a battered old jalopy drove into camp. We could hardly believe our eyes. This must be our truck, because Papa was driving it and Mamma, holding Chuckles, was sitting beside him. Where was our new canvas top? Why did this truck look more battered than the one we left Smelter City in? What in the world had happened?

Mamma, with much moaning and groaning, started climbing over the door. This wasn't unusual in itself, since to open the door required two hands and a few cusswords, and Mamma had her arms full of Chuckles and seldom used cusswords. This time it was different, because she was moaning and mumbling something about *Papa and his watch and it's a wonder any of us came out alive.* Papa was a little slower getting himself detached from the seat. He had no trouble with a door, because there was no door on his side of the car. He was grumbling something that sounded like *soft shoulders* when Mamma's voice drowned his out. They were both trying to explain what happened as they saw it. In the confusion of both of them talking at once, it was some time before we understood what caused their trouble.

The story, after being argued pro and con between Mamma and Papa and finally settled, went like this. They were going up the steep grade after crossing Dry Creek when Mamma, wondering about the time of day, reached over to take Papa's watch out of the pocket in the bib of his overalls. Papa looked down to see what she was doing, and took his eyes off the road and his mind off his driving. The car wandered over to the edge of the road and hit a soft shoulder that crumbled. Before they realized what was happening, they were rolling toward the bottom of the canyon. When Mamma came out of shock, she was gripping a big piece of the windshield in her hands, thinking it was Chuckles. Papa was shaking her and asking, "Are you all right, Mom?"

A whimpering baby cry brought them back to life at once. They found Chuckles back of the seat, unhurt but badly frightened. Mamma started looking the baby and herself over to see if they were all right. Papa, still in sort of a daze, was watching the procedure. "What are we going to do now Mother?" he asked.

Mamma looked up as though shocked that there were still problems to solve. Quickly she gained control of herself. She put Chuckles on her hip and said, "I'll go back up on the road and see if I can catch a ride back to Smelter City. You stay here and see that no one steals what is left of our car."

Mamma was never any hand to sit and wait, so she started down the road toward Smelter City. She would have made it all the way there in a couple of hours at the rate she was putting the miles behind her, if a car going toward Sedona hadn't stopped. The two men in the car thought it a little queer to find a woman and a baby all alone away out there in White Flat. When Mamma told them of her troubles, they said they would be glad to take her to get help. After climbing into the car Mamma asked the men if they would mind taking her on out to Sedona, as she had kinfolks living there who would come back and help get the truck out of the canyon.

"But Lady," spoke up one of Mamma's rescuers, "are you sure you don't want us to take you and the baby to a doctor first? Is your husband hurt at all?"

Mamma was quite upset to think they would question her judgment. "No!" she exclaimed. "There's nothing wrong with any of us. All we need is someone to help get our car out."

"Very well, we just wanted to be sure no one needed a doctor. Do you want to stop and tell your husband we are taking you to get help?" the man suggested.

"Yes, do stop," Mamma said. After stopping and talking to Papa, they drove on and reached Sedona in a short time.

George Black, an accommodating old-timer, took Mamma up to the Dry Ranch (the Dry Ranch is now

Myrtle and Roe Smith with their daughter Edith, around 1930.

known as Walter Jordan's fruit ranch). Here Mamma's niece, Myrtle Smith, and her husband Roe lived. Roe, with the help of his father, Link Smith, harnessed up their team and in a cloud of dust headed back to Dry Creek. Mamma told Myrtle she would stay with her and fix lunch. If the men got the car out and it would run, she and Papa would eat, then head back up the hill.

"The kids will be worried sick if we don't show up tonight."

Mamma and Myrtle were just getting up from the table when they heard the rattle and putt-putt of a car grinding to a stop in the yard. Myrtle tripped over a chair-leg and almost knocked Mamma over as the two of them rushed to see who it was. In those days there weren't many cars in Sedona, and the sound of a motor running would cause anyone to get excited.

"Oh! Excuse me, Auntie!" Myrtle paused in her mad rush to the door. "I'm sorry! Did I hurt you?"

"No, I'm all right. Who is it? Is it our truck?" Mamma asked, as she once more gained her balance and headed for the door.

"Yes, I think it is Uncle Albert and Papa Smith. They've got your car out," Myrtle said, all in one breath.

Papa and Link came in together. Papa said they had no trouble pulling the car up the twenty-foot slope with the team. They cranked the motor and it sputted and

Roe Smith and his mule team.

Wedding Day and an Unfortunate Occurrence

started, so they drove on down the road to see if the rest of the car was all right. Roe was following with the team. "I think the car is in good enough shape to make it back to camp," Papa said, while he was eating a bite of lunch.

It must have been after three o'clock when Mamma and Papa left Sedona. They had no trouble until they reached the steep hill at the head of Oak Creek Canyon. On the steepest curve, the old flivver coughed a couple of times and gave up. The emergency brake on the Model-Ts seldom worked by the time we acquired them. Really, the only use for it was that when the car was put in neutral the emergency brake was pulled on. If a car died on a hill, the driver held his foot on the foot brake until the passenger could put a rock in front or behind the wheel as needed, to act as a brake. If you were alone in the car, you slowly worked the car against the bank or a rock so you could take care of your trouble.

Mamma, already nervous from the accident, didn't trust Papa or the car. She jumped out with Chuckles under her arm and grabbed a big rock to poke under the wheel. After much cussing and cranking, Papa got the car started. It went a few feet and died again. This continued at about fifty feet per start, with Mamma running along carrying Chuckles and the rock; and always managing to reach the car just in time to put the rock under the wheel. They eventually reached the top of the hill in this manner. Mamma threw the rock away and climbed in, thinking their trouble was over. Much to their dismay, they found that at the slightest rise in the road, the car would balk and Mamma would have to jump out and get a rock again. They finally reached the County Road Camp at the old Pump House (now Kachina Village). Mamma's brother, Fred Thompson, was the foreman at the camp. He and his men came out to help find what was wrong with the pickup. They found some of the coils badly shot. Uncle Fred happened to have some extra coils, and after he put the new ones into the car it purred like a kitten all the way to Lake Mary.

Uncle Fred Thompson, Mamma's brother, about 1911.

CHAPTER SIX

Changing Tires

Before we left Lake Mary we developed a cough. Later we discovered all of us except our menfolks had whooping cough. They had had the disease when they were children. I don't remember it affecting me much, but it was an inconvenience. In the free campgrounds where we always stayed, the other campers wouldn't let their children come near our camp and they chased us off if we came near theirs. I guess they were afraid we would give their little darlings our cough. I did think it was a nuisance to get filled up at meal time, then start coughing and lose all that good food. I guess Mamma was quite sick and lost a lot of weight, but somehow she always managed to get our meals on time and her family tucked in at night.

A friend watches as Walter changes a tire in the late twenties; Erma can be seen looking out of window. Car is a deluxe model compared to those taken on the Purtymun trip.

Twenty-two miles east of Flagstaff we left the pine forest and in another ten miles the cedar trees disappeared. We were now crossing a high, dry plateau with very little vegetation. The mountains we had driven through could still be seen far to the south. While driving across these seemingly endless miles with the hot sun blazing down on us, there were many thankful glances toward Kenneth for his foresight in trading his old tires to his brother for almost new ones. We also were glad Kenneth and Walter had picked up those tires in the Flagstaff dump. A lot of the time we would barely make ten miles before either Papa's or Walter's car would have a flat tire.

Changing a tire back in nineteen twenty-four meant much more work than it does today. We didn't have a spare all ready to slip on. The flat tire had to be removed

Changing Tires

from the rim while the wheel was still on the car. Model-T wheels and rims were all made in one piece. If the tube had a hole in it, half the tire was taken off the rim and the tube removed. The tube patching was bought in a roll about four inches wide and a foot long. A patch large enough to cover the hole was cut from this strip. A buffer that came with the patching was used to clean the spot on the tube where the hole was. Then glue was used to stick the patch in place. If there had been a blow-out and there was a hole in the tire, a patch had to be put over this hole before the tube could be replaced. The tire patches we used came from old tires or tubes that were in such bad shape they couldn't be patched anymore. A section of an old tire was cut out and the tread separated to make it thin so it could be placed inside the tire, over the hole as a patch. We never threw a tire or an old tube away, as they could be used as patches. After the tube had been patched and put back in the tire, and the tire put back on the rim, the only thing left to do was pump up the tube inside the tire. This was done with a hand pump. Everyone helped with this job because it was tiresome for one person to push up and down on the pump handle until there was enough air in the tube.

By the time we got back to Arizona, our tires and tubes were just one big patch on top of a big patch. We bought no tires and only one tube on the whole trip. We never drove past a tire along the roadside without stopping and giving it a thorough inspection. In this way we found many a tire with a couple of hundred miles of driving left in it. I remember one in particular, which we picked up or found on the border between Arizona and New Mexico. Walter was still using that tire when we re-entered Arizona nine months later.

It never seemed to fail. We would have our flats on the most barren stretches of the road. Usually there was not a tree, bush, or even a blade of grass in sight. Erma, already riding under the only shelter we had from the blazing sun, remained in the seat of their car. Sometimes Mamma, holding Chuckles, would get in beside her. Virgie, as usual, was already riding in Erma's car or would squeeze in when we stopped. She seldom rode in the back of the truck with the rest of us kids. Poor Violet, Bud and I were left out in the sun gasping for breath and begging for water. If eventually we succeeded in getting a drink from the canteens, the water would be almost at the boiling point. Mamma always watched us as we got our drink to make sure we took no more than a sip. We never knew just how long it would take us to reach the next water, with our frequent flats and all.

CHAPTER SEVEN

Albuquerque Campground

We all remembered well the night we spent at Holbrook, on the bank of the Little Colorado River. It was there we found the first alkali water. To folks like us, who were used to good spring water, that salty, sweet, hot stuff just didn't taste like water at all. We kids raised such a fuss, Walter went over to a store and bought a few lemons with part of his small hoard of traveling funds, so Mamma could satisfy the thirst of her brood with lemonade.

After traveling so many miles across desolate hot country, it was a welcome change when leaving Springerville, to find our road starting back into the mountains. As we gained altitude we came into cedar and pinon trees. Later the pines began to show up, but we never came into a thick forest like south of Flagstaff.

One of my biggest disillusions on the trip was to find there wasn't any drastic change in the color of the ground when crossing from one state to another. I had the impression the state lines could be as plainly seen as they were on a map. When Papa said, "I guess we are in New Mexico now," I looked at him and thought he must be kidding. After several more hours of travel I became convinced we were in New Mexico, although the ground was the same color it was in Arizona.

Due to a flat tire near Pie Town in New Mexico, Virgie spent two dollars and seventy-five cents of the precious three dollars she won in an essay contest just before school was out. Not dreaming the watermelon cost so much, she picked out a big one because she knew Mamma would make her divide it with all of us. I thought it was real delicious and said so. Virgie was thinking how much it cost her when she gave me a dirty look. "It ought to be good at that price," she muttered. "I should have just bought a little one and slipped off and ate it all by myself."

Nothing unusual happened after we left Pie Town as we came down out of the mountains into the Rio Grande Valley. On the bank of the river was a little settlement we called "Scare-Crow." It was spelled Socorro. If we kids had trouble pronouncing the name of a town, we made up our own name. In this way we could identify the place if we talked about it later.

We followed the Rio Grande River north for eighty some miles to Albuquerque. Here we camped for a couple of nights in the same spot. This was quite a welcome change. I guess the reason for such a long stay was because we were on the bank of the river. When Mamma saw all that water, she ex-claimed, "We had better stop here for awhile, so I can give the kids a bath and wash a few clothes."

It was early in the evening when we parked under some big cottonwood trees in a deserted campground. Mamma began rummaging around in a clothes sack; she soon dug out clean clothes, washrags, and towels. She handed all these things, as well as a bar of soap, to my older sisters. "Take the kids down to the river and scrub them up good," she ordered. "After it gets a little darker and we get camp set up, the menfolks and I will go down and take our baths."

As none of us had bathing suits and we were intending to take baths anyway, we just stripped off our clothes and jumped in the nice cold water. Della had just turned me loose after scrubbing off most of my hide along with the dirt, when we heard Kenneth yell, "Della! Get out of the river and get your clothes on. There's a bunch of naked Mexican boys coming down the river." We looked up, but could barely see Kenneth. He was dragging what looked like half a dead cottonwood tree toward camp for the campfire.

Of all the dirty tricks: just when I was free to have some fun, we had to hurry into our clothes and follow Kenneth and his load of wood back to camp. As we trudged along through the hot sand, I couldn't help but gripe. "Why couldn't those darned Mexicans have found somewhere else to swim. We were there first."

Mamma, drawing her hands out of the soap-filled wash-tub the next morning, picked up a dirty shirt and dried her hands. She then began looking in every direction and I was sure she was looking for me. I shrunk down behind the bush beside me, because I was sure she wanted me to do some work. I couldn't see why Mamma made us change clothes and do all that washing. We weren't going anyplace special. No-body would see us anyway. We'd just get dirty all over again.

I soon found all my worry was for nothing. Mamma wasn't looking for me; she was looking for Virgie, who was sitting in Walter's car reading a book. "Virgie," Mamma called; then as she continued to look around, "Where did that kid go? Oh! There you are. I might have known you'd be poked out of sight reading a book. Get over here and help Erma hang the rest of these clothes."

Virgie marked the spot in her book and as she climbed out of the car, Mamma gave her instructions. "Help Erma hang the rest of these clothes. That fence is full so you will have to spread the rest of them on those bushes."

Just then Papa came in sight dragging a big limb off an oak tree. "I wonder what in the world your dad is dragging that old green thing up here for. He'd better get something dry if he expects me to fix dinner," Mamma said. She stacked a few twigs on the coals where the wash-boiler had been boiling away all morning. Mamma wouldn't think of using hand or dish towels, pillow cases, or any other white clothes without giving them a good boiling in soapy lye water to kill the germs.

"We'll get the wood in a few minutes, Mother," Walter said. He glanced up from the mountain of tires and tubes he and Kenneth had been working with all morning. They had succeeded in cutting half a dozen boots from old tires and had repaired many tubes to where no bubbles appeared, showing the escaping of air, when they were ducked in the river.

"I'm going to make a jack that won't take half a day to jack up a wheel," Papa grinned. He grabbed the handsaw and started sawing on the Y-shaped oak he had dragged up. Everybody looked at him and wondered what he had in mind. He spent the rest of the day peeling the limb and attaching an eight-foot pole through the crotch. Our looks turned from wonder to admiration, though, when Papa finally erected his contraption back of the truck. Hooking the short end of the pole under the axle, he pushed lightly on the other end and the whole back of the truck raised off the ground in seconds.

We had become seasoned travelers by the time we reached Albuquerque and headed north over Raton Pass into Colorado. Little things like flat tires never bothered us anymore.

CHAPTER EIGHT

The Rocky Mountain Trail

As we approached Pueblo, we noticed great fields of alfalfa that needed cutting and being made into hay. Papa steered the truck onto the side of the road and waited for the other men to join him. After talking things over, they de-cided to look for work as our money was getting low. All our men had been raised on farms, so naturally they would be looking for that type of work.

None of us dreamed of the trouble we would have as we set up camp near the Arkansas River. We chose a place near the river because it simplified the processes of cooking, washing and bathing. It was a beautiful campsite. There was plenty of shade under the big cottonwood trees and lots of wood lying on the ground. In fact, it looked as though no one had camped here in a long time. Walter and Kenneth went up to a nearby farmhouse to see about the job while the rest of us set up camp. The women had lunch ready by the time the men came back with the news that they could go to work that very afternoon, stacking hay in the field just over the fence from our camp. We decided to stay as long as the work held out, because everything seemed so convenient here.

The water didn't taste so good, but we thought we could put up with it because everything else was so nice. What a revelation: as soon as the sun went down, we found out why no one was camping in this spot. The mosquitoes came out in great swarms. They must have been starved from the way they chewed on us. The only relief we could find was to go to bed and cover up our heads. Even then, occasionally, one would crawl into our bed and nip us before we could locate him. If we hadn't been so broke we would've pulled out after that first miserable night. The men worked for four days before we decided we couldn't take any more of that horrible old river water and those mosquitoes.

The next town I remember was Colorado Springs. It was located on the eastern slopes of the Rocky Mountains and was a beautiful place. There were green lawns and pretty flowers inside white picket fences around all the fancy houses. I was hoping we would park here for awhile, but I guess Papa thought it looked too much like a rich man's town. We just drove through and went on our way toward Leadville. We did pass within seeing distance of Pike's Peak. Finding a place named Pike's Peak was quite a shock to me. All my life we had called any high point of land Pike's Peak, never even guessing there was a Pike's Peak in the country. My scholarly sister, Virgie, had probably started this name-calling, but had never bothered to explain what it meant to us.

The Fourth of July celebration was in full swing as we entered Leadville. Everyone was out in the street, all dressed up and watching a parade when we rolled into view. The parade marched up Main Street with us bringing up the rear, followed by a bunch of smart aleck kids. They were hooting and laughing and pointing at us and some of them followed us clear to the edge of town where

The Rocky Mountain Trail

we stopped to fix lunch. I didn't know why they were making such a fuss. Maybe it was because they lived in this secluded little old mining town and weren't used to seeing traveling folks like us. I sure didn't enjoy my Fourth of July lunch with those kids poking fun at our cars and clothes and everything. I guess Mamma noticed how bad we felt because she told us kids we could have enough sugar and canned milk to make snow ice cream. We could use the snow from the patches of the white stuff that remained in the shady spots all around us.

Leadville is a short distance from one of the highest passes in the Rocky Mountains. We were used to high country back in Arizona, but we were uncomfortably cold up here riding in our open-air vehicles. It was hard to believe it was July. We were all glad when we passed the Divide and started down to a lower level.

The road was narrow, and there was always a big bluff on one side and a sheer drop-off on the other. Most of the way the railroad was near our road, but at times it would disappear into a tunnel in the side of the mountain. We kids would entertain ourselves trying to see who would be the first to see the tracks when they came out of the tunnel on the other side of the mountain. One time when the tracks had disappeared and we were looking for them, we rounded a curve and saw a car on the tracks coming toward us. To folks that live near a railroad, this probably didn't seem strange, but to us country kids this was quite a sight. We hollered and squealed with excitement. As it drew near we could see the tires had been taken off the car and the rims fitted over the rails so it ran just like a train. Papa told us that the men in the car were section workers who kept the tracks repaired.

As we traveled mile after mile through these rugged mountains, we wound down into many deep canyons and crossed a lot of clear mountain streams, but none were as pretty as our own little Oak Creek Canyon. After we crossed the Divide, Papa told us all the streams we crossed would run into the Colorado River. Now I could see why the Colorado became such a big river by the time it reached our state and how it could have dug the Grand Canyon.

We were in the bottom of one of these canyons when we came upon a huge pipe coming down a steep cliff and into a big building below. When we drove by there was such a roar in the pipe and building we could hardly hear our car motors running. Papa told us it was a power station and the noise was made by water and generators making electricity. Boy, were we seeing the sights! I could just imagine how my friends' eyes would bug out when I'd get back home and tell them about all the things I had seen.

Brownie, Erma's hound, had been sick most of the way. Walter said he didn't think the dog got enough exercise, because we were on the road from daylight until dark. Mamma had said time after time, "If we'd get rid of that dog we'd all be better off. We hardly have enough food for ourselves."

In Eagle, Colorado, where we stopped for the night, Brownie was sicker than usual. He just lay around and wouldn't even eat the biscuit he was given. In the morning when we were packing to leave, Walter found Brownie had vomited and messed on the small canvas they used to cover their load with. Walter tried to clean the canvas by scraping it with a stick, but he began to gag and ended up by throwing the canvas as far as he could. Erma, knowing the necessity of even that small scrap of canvas, calmly lay the quilt she was folding on a rock. She gave Walter a disgusted look and said, "Walter, we can't throw that away. What will we cover our load with?" Then she went over and picked up the canvas and finished cleaning it.

After this incident we all realized how sick poor Brownie was, and if we continued to travel with him his chances of living were low.

Papa said, "Someone might as well kill him and get him out of his misery." Erma had been fond of the dog and we noticed tears trickling down her face as she finished packing, but she didn't say a word as we drove off leaving Kenneth behind to do the job.

A short distance from Eagle we came into a little farming community where the men went to work on a bean farm. We pitched camp at the edge of the field, where the dust was ankle deep and there wasn't a shade tree in sight. With no money for gas, we had to be near enough for the men to walk to work.

The afternoon before we moved on, Mamma took Chuckles and went up where the men were working, to pick up some of the beans the thrasher had dropped. She had given the girls orders to clean up camp and start supper. I had received permission to go swimming in a canal that wasn't far away. Of course I had to take Violet and Bud with me.

When we kids returned to camp after a very disgusting swim, I knew something was wrong with my sisters. No one would listen to my pitiful story of how we swimmers had found big old leaches sticking all over our bodies soon after we entered the water, so we had missed out on our swim. Later I overheard Della and Virgie talking about Erma starting to cry and throwing a graniteware plate at them. When Mamma or Papa left orders for my sisters to do some work, Erma would start to obey immediately. Virgie and Della were apt to fool around with something more to their liking before they would start to work. I imagine Erma had been working by herself in that terrible heat and dust and was mad because no one would help her. Either Virgie or Della had probably said something jokingly to her and she blew up and threw the plate at them.

The only thing that came out of this little squabble was that Virgie climbed into the back of our truck when we left camp the next morning. That was where she should have been riding all the time. This didn't last long though; in a few days Virgie was right back beside Erma.

When we left the bean farm we went on a navy bean diet, because it took all the money we had earned to buy gas and oil for the cars. We would have become mighty hungry if the men hadn't swiped a sack of beans before we left. To add to our misery the rainy season had begun up here. Every afternoon a shower would beat down on us. It was just such an afternoon as this, with the rain coming down harder than usual, that Papa saw a deserted looking shack near the road. He pulled over beside it, suggesting to Mamma, "Maybe we better stop here for the night and get out of the rain. We can cook a pot of our beans.

The building had only one room. It had a dirt floor and two holes where the door and window had been. Alt-

Burrell Russell (Virgie's husband-to-be), Virgie and Erma, about five years after the journey through Colorado.

hough there were many missing shakes, the steep roof took care of the rain. It would have been a nice place to spend the night if someone hadn't tacked some freshly butchered cowhides to the walls to dry. They gave the place a very unpleasant smell and look. We really hadn't much of a choice about staying here, because the rain continued to pour down all afternoon. Walter and Kenneth unloaded most of our provisions into the house while Papa built a fire with scrap lumber he found. Mamma hadn't been feeling well all day. She took an aspirin and lay down as soon as the girls finished making her bed near the door opening. We all hoped she would feel better after a rest and a good feed on the beans.

Papa had built the fire under the window opening hoping the smoke would go outside. It worked part-time, but when a puff of wind blew in the window, we all had to watch or our eyes and lungs would get filled with smoke.

We were all hungry and looking forward to a good feed on the fresh beans. After everyone had his plate and settled down to eat, we noticed Mamma had made no move to get her food. "Aren't you going to eat any supper, Mother?" Papa asked her.

"I don't like white beans very much when I'm well, let alone when I'm sick. The stink and sight of those old cowhides are enough to make one vomit without even thinking of food."

I guess getting out of the rain and a night's sleep was all Mamma needed, because in the morning she ate her bowl of oats and drank her cup of tea and was ready to move on with the rest of us. Kenneth must have not thought so, because the first town we came to the next day was a little village named Greenville. Here Kenneth suggested to Mamma that she should go to see a doctor. Mamma settled that decision quickly by stating, "We don't have enough money to buy food with, much less pay a doctor bill."

CHAPTER NINE

Parachute Creek and Narrow Escapes

When we reached Rifle, Colorado, the men found work with some very nice people. They let us camp on the lower end of their farm. It was in a pretty place on the bank of Parachute Creek, a tributary of the Colorado River. The ground was level and the shade under the big trees was a welcome treat after so many roadside camps in the sun.

The farm was located in a small valley with high mountains on either side. These mountains were covered with a peculiar shale-type rock. When these rocks were put in a hot fire and left for awhile, they would burn like chips of wood. Someone told Papa that at one time the hillside near our camp had been on fire and burned for days, before they succeeded in putting it out. I picked up one of these rocks and brought it back to Ari-

Parachute Creek and Narrow Escapes

zona with me. It was black and had scale-like markings on both sides. It looked like a section of a petrified fish.

A few years ago I read an article about these rocks. They have now developed a method of drawing oil out of them. When I read that, I wondered if those nice people who owned that farm when we were there had become rich.

Since we were going to stay here for awhile, Papa stretched the fly and even built a shelf between two trees so we would have a more convenient cupboard than just our old dish box. The kind folks the men worked for milked cows and sold cream to a creamery, and they gave us all the separated milk we could use. Mamma took advantage of this and made lots of cornstarch puddings, although we had no eggs to put in them. They sure tasted good. We had used all our home-canned fruit before we left New Mexico and had had very little dessert since. Of course, once in awhile if we had sugar enough, Papa would make sugar syrup to sop our biscuits in.

Our stay in this beautiful campsite was marred by one big evil, Rocky Mountain ticks. Different members of our clan would find ticks on themselves almost every day. One day Violet, who was a "fraidy cat," was watching Papa dig a big tick out of his leg. She pushed her hair out of her eyes so she could see better and discovered she had a tick embedded in her forehead. With a loud squeal she started running around camp. She would dodge and scream every time anyone tried to stop her insane race. Finally as she streaked past, Mamma clamped onto her arm. The big race was over and the fight ended when enough help arrived to hold her while the tick was removed.

One afternoon while we were living here, Della, the fisherwoman of our family, rigged up a fishing pole and went down to the creek hoping to catch some fish for our supper. She had only been gone a short time when we heard her scream, "Mamma, Mamma!" followed by a silence.

We were all paralyzed with fear as we let our imaginations run wild. It was a steep drop of ten feet from the bank, where Della planned on fishing, to a huge pile of rocks that gradually sloped off into a deep pond. In order to get her hook into the water, Della would have to stand on the edge of this cliff and cast her line a great distance. When we heard her scream we all pictured her losing her balance and falling onto the rocks below with either a broken back or other serious injuries. Mamma, who always seemed to know exactly what to do in an emergency, reached the spot first. There on the bank, safe and sound, sat Della almost in tears. She looked up as Mamma approached and said, "I almost had him up here on the bank when he flopped off the hook and back into the pool. Mamma, he was the biggest trout I'd ever caught."

"Well, you didn't have to scare us all half to death by screaming just because you lost a fish," Mamma said, as she turned back toward camp.

Chuckles became very sick while we were living here. He had developed a bad case of diarrhea along with his whooping cough. Mamma went up to the farmhouse and asked the nice lady if she knew of some remedy to help him. Either the strawberry leaf tea or the paregoric the lady gave to Mamma for Chuckles helped him, because he began to improve and soon was well again.

The men worked for three weeks in Rifle. When we moved on, there was enough money left, after buying our groceries and putting some away for gas and oil, to buy badly needed parts of the cars.

The old Fords had plugged along faithfully all the way from Arizona in spite of their heavy loads, the steep mountain grades, and the rains to hinder our progress. Occasionally a piece of bailing wire was brought to their

Parachute Creek and Narrow Escapes

aid. It was used to hold some worn-out part together or to replace a part that was beyond mending.

We found a camping spot out of Grand Junction near the Colorado River where we could work on the cars. Walter and Kenneth, both experienced Model-T mechanics, took over the job of putting our transportation back into tip-top shape.

Walter had jacked his car up and put blocks of wood under the axles to hold it while he worked on the brakes. He had removed the front wheels and was on his back beneath the car, when somehow he knocked it off the blocks. Kenneth was working on his car nearby when he heard a loud grunt coming from the direction of Walter's car. Kenneth whirled around and seeing nothing but Walter's legs sticking out from under the radiator, he quickly caught hold of the car and lifted it up and held it until Walter could worm his way out. By the time Walter was out from under the car, we were all gathered there. Erma, her face white and her voice almost inaudible, was beside Walter in seconds. "Are you all right?" she asked, as she and Kenneth knelt beside him.

"My God! What next is going to happen to us?" was Mamma's response as she joined Kenneth and Erma where Walter lay.

"I don't think I'm hurt bad. Just had the wind knocked out of me," Walter said as he raised himself to a sitting position.

Thank God, Walter was right. Some miracle had saved him from being seriously injured.

No one, including Kenneth, could ever figure how one man could have lifted that car and held it up long enough for Walter to get out from under it.

While we were in the valleys along the Colorado River we were in farming country. We passed big orchards of peaches, plums, apricots, and other fruit. There were fields of cantaloupe and watermelons as well as vegetable farms. The road was lined with farmhouses and green

Walter making sure the family pooch gets in the picture at a gathering later in the twenties. Grown-ups, left to right: Walter Baker, Albert and Clara Purtymun, Burrell and Virgie Russell, cousin Iva Purtymun. Kids in front row: Charley Purtymun with mouth open, Zola and Bud Purtymun, Dorothy Baker, and Ray Purtymun (Iva's boy) with hand on

fields. However, after leaving Grand Junction, except when we crossed the Green River, we were in sagebrush flats. It became very monotonous traveling mile after mile and seeing nothing but sagebrush and weeds. Sure was a good thing we had our cars repaired and no more than the usual amount of flat tires, or we might have turned around and headed back to Arizona.

Our good luck with tires ran out after the night we spent near the railroad tracks, twenty-five miles east of Price, Utah. All through the night the lonesome whistle of the trains, followed by the clicking of the rails and the rumble of the engines as the trains flew by, kept us awake. Therefore we were up, packed and rolling down the road by six in the morning. We planned on reaching Price by suppertime.

Parachute Creek and Narrow Escapes

Price is a small Mormon town at the foot of the Wasatch Mountain range. A short distance east of Price, in what is now a ghost coal mining town, Mamma's grandmother, Elizabeth James, was buried in nineteen hundred and five. We might have taken time to look for her grave if flat tires hadn't interfered. I don't think anyone knew how many flat tires we had that day. Sometimes while the men were fixing one tire, they would discover two more were flat. Although we left camp at six in the morning, we covered only three miles before darkness closed in on us once more.

Only one good thing I can remember happened that day. While the women were preparing supper in the evening dusk, a jackrabbit was unlucky enough to come hopping by camp. Papa grabbed his old shotgun and we had rabbit for supper. We'd had no meat except salt pork since leaving Arizona. I never remember anything tasting so good as that Dutch-oven fried rabbit.

It was afternoon before we moved out of this camp. The men wanted to get a new supply of tires ready for future use. Mamma decided to cook a pot of beans while we waited. It kept us kids busy dragging up sagebrush to keep the fire burning. Sagebrush burns like paper. It's not a bit like the oak we used at home when we wanted a slow, long lasting fire to cook beans.

Either the newly-repaired tires or the cooler, higher altitude where we were traveling helped our tire situation. We spent one night in Price, where the men inquired about work. They were told if they wanted to stick around for awhile, they might get work at a smelter in a nearby town. We hadn't enough money to wait, so we proceeded on up the road into the Wasatch Mountains. The road goes through a high pass here, but it was nothing like the high country we had been through while crossing the Rocky Mountains.

CHAPTER TEN

Adventures in Salt Lake City

When we reached the lower ridges on the west side of the Wasatch Mountains, we found ourselves once more in farming country. First, we passed large homes surrounded by out-buildings and big barns with neat log fences and corrals. Papa said these were cattle ranches.

As we drove north at the base of the mountains, we wandered through several very pretty little Mormon settlements. Each house was built under the shade of tall poplar trees and in the center of a prosperous-looking farm. Soon the farms and towns all ran together. There was only one street with business buildings and farms lining both sides of the road. There were no side roads, except the ones that went to each of the farmhouses.

It was getting late in the afternoon and we began looking for somewhere to spend the night. All our cars were low on gas and oil. We had no money left to buy

Adventures in Salt Lake City

anything. Our men had to put water in the crankcases as a substitute for oil, and we all started silently praying that we could find somewhere to camp before our gas ran out or it became too dark to drive. Back home, where there were only a few cars and we knew every curve of the road, we often hung a lantern in front of the radiator and went on to our destination in spite of the darkness. Our cars seldom had lights, so we used them for daylight driving only.

We had been having tire trouble all afternoon, and when our last good tube blew out the men didn't bother to fix it. They just stuffed one of the older tires with old tubes and rags to protect the rim, and we limped on down the road. Our "Grand Entrance" into Salt Lake City is probably remembered and talked about to this day by anyone lucky enough to have seen us bumping up the street. To make matters worse, the tubes and rags began coming out of the tire. They were dangling and banging against the side of the car and flying through the air at each turn of the wheel.

When we came to a road that led up to a smelter, we stopped for a few minutes to discuss applying for work there in the morning. It was now almost dark and as we drove on, Kenneth, who was in the rear, didn't see Papa turn off the main street. Papa followed a street headed in the direction of the mountains. He thought if we could only get out of town we could pull off to the side of the road anywhere to spend the night. We had traveled on up this side street some distance when Mamma, turning to stop us kids squabbling, noticed only Walter's car behind us. "Dad! What's happened to Della and Kenneth? They're not following us," she said.

Papa ground to a halt. "It's getting too dark to see to drive anyway. The kids will probably show up pretty soon. If they don't we'll have to look for them in the morning. There's nothing we can do in the dark."

There was a narrow, level strip of land between the road and the houses. Walter and Papa parked the cars and we pulled the beds out and went to sleep without supper. Kenneth was hauling one of our mattresses, so we had to double up and sleep with what we had. Rising early in the morning, we found our camping spot, which had looked so good in the dark last night, was really someone's front yard. It was a good thing most cities of any size had free campgrounds, or we might have spent more than this one night in someone's yard.

We couldn't cook breakfast here. We loaded the cars, while Papa and Walter repaired the flat tire. Mamma kept worrying, because Della and Kenneth didn't show up. Della had been sick for the last week. We didn't find the free campground until we were on the other side of Salt Lake City. It was in a small suburb of Salt Lake, called Kaysville.

After getting camp set up in our new surroundings, Papa and Walter went off on foot to look for Della and Kenneth, and for work. The womenfolks were quite sick with whooping cough or something that could have been brought on by our restricted diet. Mamma, who usually weighed one hundred and forty pounds, was down to one hundred and twenty. Chuckles, after his siege of diarrhea, weighed only twenty pounds. Virgie and Erma just lay around camp doing as little work as they could and took no interest at all in our surroundings. I was still in good shape, maybe because I always saw to it that I got a little more than my share of whatever food was available.

I guess everybody was worried because we had lost Kenneth and Della. The groceries were all in our car and the newlyweds had no money. Papa and Walter tried to console Mamma by telling her Kenneth probably found work. I felt sure Kenneth, who was strong and healthy, could take care of himself and Della. Anyway, weren't Papa and Walter doing all they could to find them?

The first day out Papa and Walter found jobs on a farm in Kaysville. As they didn't have to go to work until

Adventures in Salt Lake City

the next day, they went to all the gas stations and stores within walking distance and left the description of Della and Kenneth and their old flivver. Walter used his last dime to ride on a streetcar into Salt Lake City to look for them; all their efforts were in vain.

I liked this camp. There were a couple of girls my age a short distance from our camp. Their mother had smaller children and wasn't overly strict with the older ones. We were all more or less free to do as we pleased.

It didn't take me long to discover the apricot tree just over the fence from our camp. Of course, it was in someone's backyard, but that didn't stop me from leaning over the fence and picking a few for Bud, Violet and myself. Our two neighbor girls soon joined us. They told me the tree belonged to some crabby old lady. If I would wait until it was dark, they would join me and we would crawl under the fence and get all we wanted. The ground was covered with apricots that were already rotten. I figured we were doing the right thing by gathering what we wanted, as long as we didn't get caught.

The next morning, bubbling over with excitement and my pockets filled with apricots, I slipped away from Violet and Bud and joined my new girl friends. We had planned an exploring excursion. We soon discovered the schoolhouse, and after trying the swings, slides, and other playground things, we came upon a deserted swimming pool. It was full of moss-covered stale water that wasn't fit to swim in. We looked around until we found the valve to drain the pool and one to refill it. Filled with plans of a nice swim tomorrow, we opened the drain and headed back to camp. Much to my surprise when I reached camp, Mamma's greeting was, "Laura, have you been stealing apricots?"

I began trembling. Knowing I couldn't tell a complete lie, I said, "Well, those other girls said the lady didn't care and I only took a few."

Mamma warned me, "You better leave them all alone. The sheriff was here this morning. He wanted to know if my kids had been stealing apricots and I told him there was no one here except the little kids and Virgie. She has been lying on the bed sick all day."

Then the sheriff told Mamma that he didn't think anyone was stealing the old lady's apricots. She was always griping about something, he said, and he had to do his duty and come around to satisfy her. He also said if she was so mean that she would rather let the apricots fall on the ground and rot than give them away, he was tempted to take some himself. Maybe he considered taking some, but Mamma sure didn't. She gave me a good lecture on stealing. As a result of this episode, I didn't dare go over in that part of the campground where the apricot tree was for fear the old lady would have a gun sticking out of a window aimed at me.

After the apricot deal, I was ready to call off our swimming party the next day. It took quite a bit of coaxing to convince me this wasn't the same as stealing. I finally gave in when the girls said the pool didn't belong to a mean old lady, and after all, it probably had been built especially for kids like us to use.

Much to our surprise when we reached the pool, we found it filled with fresh water and people. We girls didn't have a bathing suit, so we lost out on our swim.

As we walked back home in the hot sun, we were filled with resentment toward those people who had spoiled our fun. We saw the mailman walking up the street putting mail in the boxes near each house. "I bet those people at the pool live in these houses," I said. "There doesn't seem to be anyone around here."

"Let's do something to get even with them," suggested one of my friends. "I'll tell you what, how's about looking in their mailboxes, and if the mailman left anything interesting, taking it?"

"Sounds like a good idea," agreed the other girl.

As soon as the mailman was out of sight, we proceeded to do just that. We were lucky. There wasn't much that attracted our attention and no one saw us or we

Adventures in Salt Lake City

might have been in a mess. The only thing we took was a magazine each. Poking the magazine under our clothes we hurried back to camp.

The girls and I had just reached camp, when Della and Kenneth in their little strip-down drove up. Erma, who was peeling potatoes, waved a half-peeled potato in the air and gave out a yell that could be heard all over the campground. "Della and Kenneth are here!"

Everybody instantly stopped whatever they were doing and came running. It would have been hard to tell who was the happiest, Della and Kenneth when they accidentally drove into the same campground we were in, or us when we recognized them and their old flivver. Kenneth jumped out of the car and rushed up to the fire where supper was cooking. "You don't have half enough food there, put some more on," he said.

After losing sight of us on the other side of Salt Lake City, Kenneth and Della continued up the main street, where they eventually found a free campground. Looking through the campground they couldn't find us. All their inquiries brought the same answer: "No! Never seen anybody like you described." They then made several trips up and down the main street, finally giving up in disgust. With darkness on their heels, they drove back to the campground to wait for dawn.

There were several cars belonging to a tribe of gypsies in this camp. The only members of the tribe at home when Della and Kenneth arrived were an old, old, dried-up woman and a small boy. The boy's job was to stand with a tree branch and keep the flies off the old woman. There were plenty of flies, too. The outhouse was quite some distance from the gypsies' camp, so just before dark the little boy had to help the old woman to a nearby chair with a hole cut through the seat, so she could answer her call of nature. This chair was in the center of the camp, in sight of anyone who happened to be looking in that direction.

Della said, "We were both relieved when darkness

came and the boy was released from his tedious task. It also helped to hide some of the filth in that camp."

With neither money nor food, the Greenwells proceeded to bed down for the night. Before they could get their bed made, another jalopy pulled into camp and the man came over to swap travel tales with his Arizona neighbors. When he heard of their bad luck he invited them over to his camp for supper. Della said she was so sick she would just go to bed. Kenneth, who never refused to eat, accepted the invitation. These kind folks were almost as hard up as Della and Kenneth. All they had to eat were crackers and tea. After Kenneth had drank the tea and ate a few of their crackers, he discovered they had used water for their tea from the only cooking vessel they owned. This kettle was used for a dishpan, a washbasin, a bathtub or any other purpose they saw fit. Kenneth came back to Della feeling almost as sick as she. We may have been as poor as those people, but at least we tried to be sanitary.

The next morning they started looking for us again. Kenneth found a dime in his pocket, so he bought a box of cookies for their breakfast. They then headed back toward the smelter. They were sure Papa and Walter would be there looking for work. They had almost reached the smelter, when the motor of their car began knocking and making such a racket that Kenneth knew they had burned out a rod. After all, water was never intended to replace oil as a lubricant. Kenneth pulled over to the side of the road where, luckily, there was a big oak tree for shade. He made Della as comfortable as possible, then walked on to the smelter. He asked about work and inquired if Papa and Walter had been seen there. Much to his disappointment, they weren't hiring anyone and no men answering Papa's and Walter's description had been seen around.

Not knowing what else he could do, after getting back to Della, Kenneth walked on to Salt Lake City. He asked for work at every likely-looking spot, but received the

Adventures in Salt Lake City

same answer. "There's more men looking for work around here than there's jobs." It was late when Kenneth got back to the car. He was too tired and hungry to care about anything except rest and sleep. Della was still so sick she did little but sleep. Her fever became so high her hair began coming out. Luckily, later on it came back in curly.

By morning they were getting desperate. As a last resort they decided to see if they had anything they could hock. Kenneth pulled a ring that was a birthday gift from his finger. To this they added their box of silverware, a wedding present. Della looked through her hope chest of embroidery and crochet work. She picked the most attractive pieces for him to sell or hock.

Once more, loaded down with this merchandise, Kenneth started down the road toward Salt Lake City. He had seen a pawnshop there and felt sure he could get a little money out of some of these things. A man walking ahead of Kenneth stopped and picked up a half-eaten apple in the gutter and started chewing on it. Kenneth had passed this apple yesterday and had thought about eating it himself. This gave Kenneth courage, as he figured that man must be hungrier than he was.

The pawnshop gave Kenneth three dollars for his ring and the silverware. After selling several pieces of Della's fancy work, Kenneth had enough money to buy a new connecting rod and oil and gas for the car.

On his way back to the car Kenneth had to pass a bakery shop. He had been without food for over twenty-four hours. The smell of the baking and the display of all that food was too much for him to resist. He went and bought a dozen doughnuts. There were only two doughnuts left in the sack by the time he came to a garage where he purchased the connecting rod and the oil. After leaving the garage, Kenneth fought temptation all the way back to Della with the two doughnuts still uneaten. Della was still not hungry. She managed to eat one of the doughnuts and gave the other one back to Kenneth.

After they had crawled into bed that night, a lady who

had heard their story came by and gave them fifty cents.

In the morning, with the hope of getting something to eat soon, Kenneth went to work on the car. He replaced the connecting rod, and with a hind wheel jacked up he started cranking the old bus. No amount of cranking seemed to bring even one little putt out of the engine. There was only one thing left to do. They would have to find someone to pull them until the car started. The first man Kenneth stopped was willing to do the job, but he had no tow chain. Kenneth solved that problem by dragging out his supply of bailing wire. He made a cable of sorts out of the bailing wire and connected the two cars together. With the quick jerk it took to get the car rolling, the wire snapped and the man drove off leaving Kenneth's car still sitting under the tree.

"I'm not going to let a little thing like a wire breaking stop us," Kenneth said to Della. "I'll fix the next one so it won't break loose from our car."

He then climbed out of the car and picked up a good-sized limb under the tree, and with skill he wired it to the front of the car. Once more he stopped a friendly-looking guy, who said he would give them a pull. This time, with the limb acting as a tow bar, they hung together until their flivver started. Kenneth unhooked the cars and thanked the guy.

At last they were free to move on down the road. As they were driving along, they passed a furniture store with a huge stack of mattresses on display. That gave Kenneth an idea: he remembered he was hauling one of our mattresses. "Why not sell the old man's mattress? We will probably not see them again until they get back to Arizona," he said. "Maybe we can get enough money out of it to feed us until I can get a job."

Della said it would be all right with her. The next second-hand store they came to Kenneth stopped, only to find it was against the law to sell second-hand mattresses in Utah.

Adventures in Salt Lake City

Kenneth stopped to ask for work at every place he had missed in his former trips into Salt Lake City. Finally, someone told him there was a chance he could get work at some of the farms out in Kaysville.

That is how it happened they stopped in the Kaysville campground where we were camped.

Walter and Papa were already working when Kenneth and Della found us. Our cars needed overhauling because of the water we had put in the crankcases, so Kenneth took over that job.

Another highlight of our stay in Kaysville was what happened the night we tried to watch a play through the open door and windows of a church. The church was on the street side of our campground. We kids seldom missed anything that was within seeing distance of our camp.

We noticed an unusual amount of activity going on at the church and many people decked out in their best clothes were coming from every direction. We thought maybe there was going to be a wedding.

As soon as things quieted down and everyone was in the church, we crept up close so we could look in. It was a mighty hot night and they had opened all the windows and left the door open. After seeing the fancy costumes, the false wigs and beards, and the long garbs, we knew they were going to have some kind of religious play.

Virgie, giving orders as usual, said, "Laura, go back to camp and tell the rest of the gang about the play. Maybe they would enjoy it too."

This play looks like it might be something great, I was thinking as I went back to camp. We had all seen silent motion picture shows after we moved to Smelter City, but here the actors were real live people, all dressed up and acting the parts. I told myself, *this probably will be as good as the play I've heard Mamma tell of seeing in Jerome.* That was when she and Aunt Lizzy, her older sister, were young girls. They were spending a week with their schoolteacher. In that play, Mamma said, there was a fight and someone got shot. When the gun went off with a bang and the man collapsed on the stage, Aunt Lizzy jumped up and said, "Let's get out of here, Clara." She grabbed Mamma's hand and pulled her up and they rushed out of the theater and back to the teacher's house.

When I told Mamma how wonderful the play was going to be, the womenfolks came back with me. We had just seated ourselves comfortably in front of the door when someone closed the door. This discouraged the grown-ups and they went back to camp. We kids moved to new seats in front of the windows. We had hardly sat down again when a man came out and told us to go away and stay away from the windows. From his tone of voice we knew we had better obey, so we went back to camp grumbling about the way we had been treated.

I always thought religious folks were supposed to be good to kids. Those people weren't. We weren't hurting anything, and they wouldn't even let us watch their old play through the window.

We stayed in Kaysville a couple of weeks, but left without seeing the Great Salt Lake or any of the other famous sights. On the whole trip we never had money or time to see anything that wasn't on the road we were traveling. It seemed we always had a town down the road set as our goal, and as soon as we reached that town we would pick a new one farther on. We would then head for it at full speed until our money gave out or a car broke down.

CHAPTER ELEVEN

Unwelcome in Wagner

As nearly as I can figure out our next destination was Pocatello, Idaho. I can't recall anything spectacular happening in that town, but just out of Pocatello we crossed the Snake River on a bridge that was the highest suspension bridge in the world at that time. This was the only wonder worth mentioning we had taken the time to look at since we left Arizona. It cost no money and because we had to cross the bridge anyway, we stopped long enough to read the sign telling about it.

I was real surprised when I found out that the tiny thread I could see at the bottom of that deep canyon was a big river. From where we were, it looked like a little irrigation ditch that I could jump across. I tried to think how I could describe this stunning sight to all those dumb kids I had left back in Arizona.

Near Twin Falls, Idaho, in a small town called Curry, we found ourselves once more broke and almost out of gas. Here we heard about some roadwork, but both the headquarters and the work were at Wagner, some forty miles off our intended route, and in Nevada. We left Curry in the afternoon and the cars sucked the last of the gas out of their tanks when we were within walking distance of our destination.

We parked beside the road in the most desert-looking sand heap I had ever seen. Not even sagebrush or cactus were dumb enough to try to live here. Mamma said if the men found work, we would find a better place to camp in the morning. We had our many canteens of water, and luckily, we had a few sticks of wood with us, or we would have had to eat a cold supper with nothing to drink. Mamma managed to keep the fire going long enough to cook some fried bread and warm the beans.

While supper was being prepared, the menfolks trudged through the sand to where we could see some tents and shacks in the distance. They figured if they were hired, they might be able to work in the morning.

Mamma had just filled the little kids' plates to get them out of the grown-ups' way when we saw the men returning. Kenneth was the first one to arrive with the news. We could tell something had gone wrong by the way he came stomping through the sand, and it didn't take us long to find out what it was. He was really raving; "Of all the dirty tricks, sending us away off down here in this sand hole and then telling us they won't hire anyone with a car."

"I can't say I'd blame them much for such a rule," Walter said, as he and Papa drifted into camp. "I don't see how they could possibly get anyone to stay in this God-forsaken desert if they had any means of getting away."

The wind was blowing when we arrived, but now it had turned into a regular gale. In most places the wind dies down as the sun sets, but it didn't here. It seemed to gain strength. The women could hardly hang onto the quilts as they tried to make the beds in the sand.

"Well, what are we going to do now?" I heard Papa say. "No work, because we have cars. We can't leave, because we have no money to buy gas. The gas in all the cars put together wouldn't take one car more than a mile up the road."

"Don't let the gas problem worry you," Kenneth said. "I saw quite a few pieces of equipment parked over there. Some of it is bound to have gas."

We kids were put to bed before it was dark enough for Kenneth and Walter to venture out in search of gas. I had covered my head to keep the blowing sand out of my eyes, but after awhile my curiosity got the better of me. I uncovered my head, because I was afraid I might miss something that was happening. Sure enough, Della and Erma were sitting on the Bakers' bed talking in low voices. I heard Erma say, "Do you hear dogs barking over there where the men went? I sure hope they don't arouse someone. Do you think if Walter and Kenneth get caught they might be put in jail?"

"I wasn't thinking about that. I was worried someone might shoot them or those dogs tear them to pieces," whispered Della.

I hadn't heard the dogs barking, but now I did. That was all I needed to make me completely forget about the wind and the sand. I lay there thinking about all the things that might happen to us. Maybe those dogs would come down and kill all of us. I got out of bed with the excuse that I had to go to the toilet, and no one could get me back into bed until the men arrived with all the containers filled with gas.

Kenneth just laughed when he heard that Della and Erma had been worried about them. "We weren't about to get caught. Those dogs were barking long before we got near there. They probably bark at the moon all night, so those people don't pay attention to them."

We all slept extra warm that night, as we were buried under six inches of sand by morning. Papa was up before daylight poking at us through the sand, because he wanted to head out of there before anyone discovered we had taken the gas.

I have traveled down that road several times in the last decade. I found the town named Curry, from where we started this unforgettable excursion. It had become part of Twin Falls; but I could never find anyone that remembered a place called Wagner. I wonder if somehow it could have blown away; or maybe it has just been buried in the sand.

CHAPTER TWELVE

Stalking a Cornfield

When we once more were traveling down our chosen path, our gas lasted until we reached Eagle, several miles north of Twin Falls, Idaho. It was just a small place with a post office and a general store. In the surrounding country there were orchards and fields of potatoes, beans, and hay. It looked like a good place to find farm work.

We were now out of flour to make our bread, so Mamma dug a souvenir dime from among her few personal belongings. She spent it for a loaf of bread because her family was hungry.

With the many mouths to be fed, the one loaf of bread was doled out, so that each person received his share. Of course the menfolks got more than the rest of us, because they were going job hunting as soon as the meal was over.

After finishing his skimpy meal, Papa went over to our pickup and pulled his old shotgun from the rack behind the seat. Looking over at Mamma for approval he said, "I wonder if I could trade this for a sack of flour over at the store?"

Mamma told him to go ahead and take it over to the store. "After all," she said, "we do have to have bread. I don't know what we will do if you men don't find work here." Then she added, "I suppose they will let you buy the gun back if you get some work."

When Kenneth returned from his job-hunting among the farms, he hurried into camp all excited. "I ran into a corn patch over there with the ears just waiting to be pulled. If someone'll go with me to help carry it back, we'll have fresh corn for supper. Sure would be nice to have a change from those darned white beans."

Della said, "I wish I felt like going for the walk. I better not try it, though, or you might have to carry me back as well as the corn. Virgie don't seem to be doing much but reading. Maybe she'll go with you."

Della's fever had finally broken, but she was still weak. Mamma was sure Della had typhoid when she was sick for so long. After all, we all should have caught something from that water we drank and the mosquito bites we received when we were camped on the Arkansas River in Colorado.

Virgie, not able to think of an excuse, had to go with Kenneth. They reached the field just before dark. Virgie was beginning to tremble for fear they would get caught, but not Kenneth. He was only thinking how good the corn would taste, as he plowed through the cornstalks making as much noise as a herd of cows. He was throwing corn to the right and left and hollering for Virgie to pick it up. Virgie was becoming more and more frightened. She was seriously thinking of ducking behind one of the rows of corn and running for camp, but in the nick of time Kenneth decided he had pulled enough and he started gathering up the ears of corn and stacking them in her arms.

On the way back to camp Virgie wanted to creep along beside the railroad tracks where they would be partly hidden by the cornfield and brush. She was running from one clump of bushes to the next, when Kenneth said, "That's foolish and takes too long. Come on up here on the railroad tracks where it is better walking and we'll reach camp in no time."

That is just what they did. They marched back to camp in plain sight of anyone that happened to be looking in their direction.

We had fresh corn for supper and I can tell you it was sure good, but I don't think Virgie enjoyed it as much as the rest of us. She was still a little shook up over the trip to the cornfield.

CHAPTER THIRTEEN

Home in a Potato Cellar

Although the men didn't find work that first day, Papa had succeeded in trading his shotgun for a sack of flour, so we had our good old Dutch oven biscuits for breakfast.

Kenneth and Walter were busy working on our car. It had been plugging along on only one cylinder when we pulled into this camp. Papa was sitting on the running board, cutting old tires into sections to be used as boots for patching the holes in some of our better tires. The women were busy cleaning camp and washing the breakfast dishes, while the little kids and I were entertaining ourselves playing hop-scotch. We all heard the awful commotion up the road at about the same time. We heard men cussing, horses stomping, harnesses jingling and we could see the dust boiling up.

Not knowing what to expect, Mamma dropped the pan she was washing and started yelling for us kids to get into the truck. She grabbed Chuckles and we all scampered to safety. We made it just in time. A team of runaway horses hit the camp. They knocked over a box or two before Papa, Walter and Kenneth managed to surround and halt them long enough for their owner to arrive and catch them.

After thanking our folks for stopping his runaways, the man noticed the mess his horses had made with the boxes; there were clothes and stuff scattered everywhere. He offered to pay for the damage that had been done.

Papa said, "I don't think your horses did any permanent damage, but if you could tell us where we could find some work, we would appreciate that."

"By Jove! I think I could use a couple of you myself. I have a big field of hay down, and by the way those clouds look, I may have trouble getting it in the barn before it gets rained on."

Then lowering his eyes after cloud gazing, he looked over to where our beds and boxes were lying on the ground with no protection from a storm. He added, "Why don't you move over into our community potato cellar? It is just across the road. There are several families living there now, but there is room for one more family."

We were all glad to move into the shelter of the potato cellar if there was a chance it might come a rain.
I thought living in a potato cellar was a wonderful experience. As near as I can remember, the cellar was an adobe building with a sod roof. It was about one hundred feet long and thirty feet wide. The side walls were only four or five feet high, but it had a driving area through the center high enough to take care of a truck loaded with potatoes. The storage bins for the potatoes were built on both sides of the driving area and were separated by huge timbers that supported the roof. The only openings in this building were the large doors at both ends. The doors were the only source of light, and were never closed while we were living there. Since the potatoes hadn't been dug in this vicinity, there were only a few sacks of year-old potatoes stored in the center bins.

It was in the empty potato bins that we made our beds.

The other campers in the cellar were all adults and worked during the daytime. They were all camped at one end, so we had the other end all to ourselves.

There was only dirt for a floor, so we built our campfire half inside and half outside the building. In this way the fire was protected from the rain and a portion of the smoke went outside.

We parked our pickups down the center aisle of the cellar and Della and Kenneth slept in their car. We used our tail-gate as a sort of cook table.

The outhouse was located a short distance from our end of the potato cellar. There was an onion patch near the outhouse, but it was on the other side of a fence. Virgie developed the habit of crawling through the fence and stuffing a few of these onions into her bloomer legs every time she went to the outhouse.

The onions tasted mighty good with our white beans, and occasionally we could talk Mamma into frying some of the onions with a few of the potatoes out of the bins.

Mamma had been brought up with the feeling that it was wrong to steal, and unless someone took the potatoes and onions and put them in with our groceries, you couldn't get her to touch them. After they were mixed with our groceries for awhile she began to feel that they were ours. Potatoes had always been Mamma's favorite dish, so by working this system, she could be persuaded to eat them.

South of the potato cellar there was a huge orchard. We could reach it by going down a long lane that was lined on both sides with a tall hedge of thorny bushes, probably planted to protect the orchard from unwelcome fruit pickers. Most of the fruit had been picked, except for a few peaches that were probably too green at the time the rest were picked.

One day as I was strolling down this lane I came to a gate that had been left open. Looking through the gate I could see a big, ripe peach in a tree nearby. It sure looked delicious. The longer I stood there looking at it, the better it looked, and my mouth began to water. I thought, *I will slip in and get just that one peach.* I cautiously crept to the tree, climbed the limb and grabbed the peach. Jumping to the ground, I quickly ran outside the gate before I even took one bite. The beating of my heart was like a drum in my ears as I pushed back against the thorny hedge and sank my teeth into the most luscious peach I ever bit into.

After eating the peach and licking the juice from my fingers, I thought, *that peach wasn't so hard to get. I think I'll go back to camp and get a sack and pick a few more.* Back in camp I found an empty salt sack, and after poking it into my pocket I hurried down the lane.

The sun had gone down and the shadows of the hedge and the fruit trees almost completely hid me as I peeked around the gate looking for a tree with enough fruit to fill my sack. I didn't want to climb too many trees for fear of getting caught. At last I spotted just what I was looking for. It was a short distance from the gate, and I could see half a dozen peaches I could reach by climbing just one limb.

Quickly I ran to the tree and up the limb. I had all the peaches in the sack and was ready to climb down, when I happened to see a movement under a nearby tree. Turning my head I could see a man standing only a short distance from me. My sack of peaches slipped from my hand and I fell to the ground. I started for the gate on all fours, before I took the time to get to my feet. In my excitement I turned down the lane in the wrong direction. I had gone some distance before I realized my mistake. I was afraid to go back by the gate, as I was sure that man would be waiting there to grab me. I had never been this far down the lane before and I didn't know how to get back to camp without passing the gate.

I crawled up in the hedge as far as I could with the stickers poking me from all sides. I squatted down, hoping I would look like part of the hedge if that man came down the lane looking for me. I was almost afraid to breathe, because with every breath I shook the leaves on the hedge and they rattled so loud I was sure anyone near could hear them. As I sat there trembling, my back began to itch and a thorn was sticking into the skin of my neck; but I didn't dare move until I was sure no one had followed me to my miserable hiding place. It seemed I sat there for hours, expecting at any minute to hear footsteps coming in my direction.

At last it became so dark I could hardly see the hedge across the lane. I crept out of the hedge as quiet as I could and tiptoed back up the lane past the gate. From there I knew I could make it to the safety of my family.

Into the lower end of the cellar I came panting. I darted around the other campers and their junk. When I reached our end of the cellar, I collapsed on one of our beds to get my breath.

Everything looked normal here. Mamma was putting the little kids to bed and Papa was stirring up the fire with a stick. The rest of the gang were going about their affairs as unconcerned as could be. They didn't seem to realize I had just barely escaped with my life.

Virgie came over to flop down on our bed and discovered me. "Oh! I didn't know you were here," she said. "The last we heard of you, one of the other campers said he saw you heading for Arizona."

Then Kenneth popped up with, "The way you are panting, you must've run clear to Arizona. How's things at home?"

Mamma knew how I felt, because she turned on the rest of them and scolded. "Oh, cut it out. She's about half scared out of her wits, so quit teasing her." Turning to me she said, "Here's your sack of peaches. The man that scared you was only one of the other campers. He was down there taking peaches himself and he had no business scaring you and then coming up here to brag about it. I hope this will teach you a lesson. You know it is wrong to steal."

CHAPTER FOURTEEN

The Great Flood

Mamma was always telling about the day we awoke to a downpour of rain. The men couldn't work in the rain, so they were all home. Mamma was cooking a big pot of white beans, our old standby, and the smoke from the fire seemed to drift into our eyes no matter where we went in the cellar.

We kids were having a very boring time. We weren't allowed out in the rain, and it seemed every way we turned we were bothering some of the grown-ups. Suddenly I thought of a way to entertain myself and the little kids too.

I had always dreamed of becoming a great singer some day. Quite often back home during the long winter evenings, our family would pass the time away singing from a church or schoolbook. Sometimes two of us would do a duet or sing a favorite song by ourselves. We had also spent many wonderful evenings singing around our campfire since we had started traveling. On these occasions I always sang my best; and I thought it was a shame to waste a beautiful voice like mine just singing to my family.

I gave each of the little kids a stick to beat out the time on an old washtub I had picked up in a nearby garbage pile. The kids were supposed to be my orchestra while I sang; but somehow they didn't seem to understand their part, because they joined me in my singing.

Our voices were echoing from one end of the cellar to the other as we practiced the two most popular songs of the day. They were "Barney Google" and "It Ain't Goin' to Rain No More."

After about a half hour of this noise I guess Mamma reached the end of her endurance, because she screeched, "If you kids don't cut out that racket I'll go completely crazy, what with this smoke in my eyes and my head splitting open with a headache."

We might have lowered our voices a little and continued our singing, but Papa came over and told us to put the tub outside and find another way that was less noisy to entertain ourselves. We knew we had to give up our music then, as no one ever disobeyed Papa.

The rain continued for the rest of the day and was still coming down hard when we went to bed that night. A little after midnight, Virgie, with whom I shared my bed, turned over and one of her hands dangled over the side of the mattress. She woke up startled when she found her hand in water.

"Papa! There's water in here!" she yelled.

Papa, who was still about half asleep, mumbled, "It's rained so much today you're imagining there's water."

"No I'm not, there's water beside our bed. Light the lantern and you'll see," answered Virgie.

Papa dug a match from under his pillow, where he always kept matches for night use, and soon he had the lantern lit. Sure enough, there was a big stream of water running in through one corner of the cellar and forming a lake around our bed.

Mamma took one look at the situation and started giving orders as she hurried into her clothes. "Virgie, get

The Great Flood

Laura out of that bed so we can pull it out of the water. Dad, light the other lantern so we can see what we are doing in here, then you and Kenneth git outside and see where this water is coming from." Kenneth, like Mamma, had his clothes on and was on the job before most of us were thoroughly awake.

Mamma seemed to be everywhere at once. She had started putting things into boxes. "Maybe we better get our stuff together and get ready to pull out of here," she said.

We had our car almost loaded and were beginning to poke boxes into the Greenwell car around Della, who was still trying to find her clothes so she could get dressed.

Mamma kept telling Della to hurry. At last Della found her dress, and while slipping it over her head she grumbled angrily, "I bet Kenneth and Papa will find where the water's coming from and we'll just have to unpack all this stuff again. Besides, it's still pouring down outside. We're as well off in here getting wet from the bottom up as we would be outside getting it from both directions."

"Oh, yeah! You should talk, sleeping in the back of that car. Why don't you trade beds with Laura and me, then maybe you'd get a little motion in you." This remark was from Virgie, who was usually as slow as Della; but due to the fact it was her bed that was floating, Virgie had managed to get into her clothes and was helping Mamma and Erma drag stuff out of the water.

"Hell, it isn't anything but a damn gopher," yelled Kenneth as he and Papa rushed back into the cellar. "The damn thing tunneled too close to the ditch and now we have most of the ditchwater coming in here."

An irrigation ditch ran along one side of the potato cellar, but was on a slightly higher level. If the ditch ran over or a hole broke through the side of it, the water would run toward the potato cellar.

Papa and Kenneth both were soaked to the skin. Neither of them had taken the time to look for a coat. Papa had pulled his bib overalls on, but forgot to put on his top shirt. His underwear had caught the full impact of the rain and was stretched across his back like a wet dishrag.

"We'll need the shovel. Anybody know where it is?" asked Papa as he bobbed around looking for the shovel. Water was pouring out of the brim of his old felt hat. Papa's hat was always the first article of clothing he put on when we were out camping.

"I saw it leaning against the post back of your truck, Dad," Walter said. "I'll go out with Kenneth and take care of the ditch. You look like you've had enough wetting for one night."

Walter was still trying to find one of his shoes. Like Della, he was a slow starter.

Our family was divided into classes, one very slow and the other very fast. The slow ones outnumbered the fast ones about five to one. The only fast ones were Mamma, Erma and Kenneth.

The children grown-up. Left to right: Zola, Bud, Violet, Laura, Virgie and Della in the mid-forties.

The Great Flood

Kenneth and Walter stopped the flood by damming the gopher hole. Most of the night was gone and everybody was wide-awake, so we just built a fire and spent what was left of the dark hours trying to dry our stuff.

Soon after the flood in the potato cellar Kenneth and Walter found a job stacking beans for a stingy old guy. He expected them to work from daylight until dark for a measly two dollars a day. They had worked for several days and they both were in the mood to quit their jobs, when just after sun-down their boss turned a flock of chickens into the field where they were working. The chickens were scurrying this way and that after grasshoppers and bugs. The men were having trouble stacking the beans without stabbing one of the chickens.

When Kenneth accidentally stuck his pitchfork into a good-sized fryer, he said, "Hell! I guess we will just have chicken for supper." He caught the chicken and had its neck wrung before it could let out a squawk.

Walter knew one chicken couldn't possibly be enough to feed our size family. He threw his pitchfork at another fryer. He knocked the chicken down, but it was only slightly wounded and so it ran off squawking. Walter tried to catch it but it ran amongst the other chickens and they all started making a racket.

Walter was still chasing the wounded chicken when the farmer came out of the barn to see what was disturbing his chickens. He fired both men, and when he paid their back wages he deducted the price of the chickens and wouldn't even let them have the fryers.

I guess Mamma was right when she told me, "If you steal something you have to pay for it some way."

After the chicken-stealing episode, our menfolks decided we had enough money left, even after Papa redeemed his shotgun, to take us a few more miles down the road toward our promised land.

It seemed Walter and Kenneth didn't want to be forced back on the white bean diet again, so before we left the potato cellar they put a sack of the cellar potatoes into the back of our truck.

CHAPTER FIFTEEN

Prune-Pickers in the Orchard

Papa was in the lead and as we pulled out onto the highway, he looked back to see if the other flivvers were started. We noticed a car was passing both Kenneth's and Walter's car and it pulled in behind us. Papa had been all shook-up ever since the boys were fired for stealing the chickens. He immediately came to the conclusion now that the man driving the car had seen Kenneth and Walter put the sack of potatoes into our car, and he was after us. Papa was so upset he turned our car onto the first side road we came to. When the car that was following us turned onto the same road, Papa said to Mamma, "I guess we might as well stop and give the potatoes back."

Papa pulled to the side of the road and stopped. What a surprise we had. The car that was following us drove right on by us and on down the road without so much as a glance in our direction.

In a short time Kenneth pulled up beside us and asked, "Where the heck you think you're going? You aren't on the right road."

"I know it," Papa said, "but I thought that guy behind me was after that sack of potatoes you two put in my car. When I turned onto this side road and he followed me, I de-cided I'd better stop and give the potatoes back."

Our next stop was at Boise, the capital of Idaho,

Prune-Pickers in the Orchard

where our whole family found jobs picking prunes. We had never had any experience picking prunes before. The only prunes I had seen were dried. Back home we would buy them in wooden boxes, twenty-five pounds at a time. I always thought prunes were just dried plums. Our plum trees at home were short and we were able to pick the fruit by either climbing the trees or standing on the ground. Here the prune trees were so tall we had to use fifteen-foot ladders, and we weren't allowed to climb the trees at all.

We were all issued prune-picking aprons that hung around our necks. The aprons had a big pocket across the front to hold the prunes. It sure was a job climbing a fifteen-foot ladder and stretching out into space to reach the prunes. We had to be careful when we came down to the ground or we would squash the prunes against the ladder.

We had worked in the prune orchard for a week and were all disgusted with this way of making our living. It was four o'clock that day when the boss from the packing shed came out and began looking over our boxes of prunes under the trees. As he walked along he made a sarcastic remark to each of us. Our boxes weren't full enough, there were too many leaves, or the prunes were smashed.

He reached the tree where Erma and Walter were picking. Walter was standing on the top of a ladder trying to keep his balance while he stretched to get hold of a limb almost out of his reach.

The man stood for awhile staring at the boxes of prunes Erma and Walter had picked before he exploded with, "Why the hell don't you cut the tree down and send it over to the packing shed? You have more sticks and leaves in these boxes than prunes."

Walter was the one member of our family who seldom lost control of his temper. As he looked down at the angry red face of the man, Walter started climbing slowly to the ground. He took his picking apron off and laying it on a box of prunes he quietly said, "You won't have to worry about any more prunes that I pick. I'm quitting right now. You will have to find someone else to listen to your gripes."

Della was the only one who objected to our leaving the prune-picking job. She had just started working at the big boss's house doing inside work. She was supposed to get all her meals up there.

If I had been in her place I probably would have hated to move on too. She would probably have had meat and dessert every meal up there.

Somewhere down the road after we left Boise I developed the only severe headache I ever had in my life. I don't think anybody could have endured, without crying, the pain I was compelled to go through as we jolted down that rough dirt road. No one realized how hard I was trying to be brave and suffer alone, but at last I reached the end of my endurance. My eyes filled with tears and my mouth flew open and I began to howl.

After listening to my squalling for a few miles, Mamma asked Papa to stop the car. "Get the canteen, Dad, and I will give her an aspirin. Maybe it will shut her up.

Papa pulled the car to the side of the road and Mamma, who never carried a purse, rummaged around in the boxes in the back of our truck until she came up with the aspirin. I swallowed it with a big gulp of water and then I lay down, hoping the aspirin would relieve my pain and maybe I could go to sleep.

Before I reached the sleeping stage my stomach began to hurt and I vomited all over everything. Papa had to stop the car again so Mamma could take care of the mess I had made. I asked Mamma for another drink of water so I could rinse my mouth and throat. She gave me a drink and we started on.

We had gone only a short distance when my head started aching and I started crying again. This time I tried my best to stick my head over the side of the pickup when I was sick, but I still didn't quite make it, so we had to stop again and wash me and the blanket.

This continued for many miles and each time we stopped I would beg for just a little water. Mamma tried to talk me out of drinking because she was sure I would get better if I would let my stomach remain empty.

I guess I was a comical sight. At least that was the way I affected Della and Kenneth, who were following close behind us.

My hair, which was always unruly, was now sticking up in every direction, because of my rolling around in the back of the truck.

Della said later that all she could see of my face was a big hole where my mouth was supposed to be. Around the hole the dust had collected in my tears. Above this my hair was sticking up like a thicket of brush. She began to laugh and told Kenneth my mouth reminded her of a cave in the side of a mountain.

Through my tears I could see they were both laughing. I knew they were laughing at me so I began to cry louder than ever. I guess I must have cried myself to sleep, because the next thing I knew we were parking for the night. Violet told me we had crossed the Snake River again, and I heard Papa tell Mamma we were probably in Oregon now.

Papa told us last night we were probably in Oregon. This doesn't look like the Oregon I'd dreamed about so many nights since we started on this trip. We're still in sagebrush. There couldn't be sagebrush in Oregon. I'm sure Oregon looks like Oak Creek Canyon and not this flat country. I can see some mountains way up ahead of us. Maybe that's where Oregon is.

These thoughts were going through my mind as we slowly worked our way to the foothills of the Blue Mountains.

CHAPTER SIXTEEN

Water

From where we camped that night I could see ridge after ridge of mountains piled high into the sky in the direction our road was taking us. I asked Papa if that wasn't Oregon up in those mountains.

"I told you last night, we're already in Oregon," he said. Papa looked a little startled when I said, "But there's sagebrush here."

"Oh yeah," he answered, "a lot of eastern Oregon is dry. The part of Oregon you're thinking about must be in the Cascade Mountains or along the Columbia River. Didn't you learn anything in school?"

I guess I had studied about Oregon in geography, but I didn't take any interest in it. I figured Oregon was so far away it didn't make any difference if I learned about it or not, because I'd never go there anyway.

We had spent a lot of time gaining altitude in the Blue Mountains and had stopped for lunch one day in a clump of pine trees. As usual I wandered off to explore while lunch was being cooked. I could see no more mountains above us, so I guessed we were at the top. I thought we were on a large mesa that would take us several hours to cross. Much to my surprise, when I came out of the trees I discovered our road was winding down the steep side of the mountain I was standing on, to a valley a long way down but almost directly below me.

The valley I was gazing at reminded me of one of Mamma's old patchwork quilts. As far as I could see there were farms. Some of the farms were square while others were oblong or other shapes. These farms were as many different colors as they were shapes. I guessed that some of the farms were only plowed fields and were just the color of the dirt, while others were different shades of green. Some of the places were a light yellow color, as a field of corn with only the dried stalks left standing. I could see in one area many houses close together where I thought a town was located. I thought the scene was really worth looking at, so I ran back to camp to tell the gang.

Do you know what? They were all so busy eating they weren't the least bit interested in going with me to see the sight. All Mamma said was, "You better get your plate and eat so we can be on our way."

Just before the sun went down we reached the valley I had seen when we were high in the Blue Mountains.

Papa parked the pickup near a small stream where we would spend the night. As soon as the car stopped rolling I was out and heading for the water. Someone had hauled in gravel and spread it across the stream to make a firm road-bed. Above the crossing a small lake had formed. I was so occupied with my wading in the cool water I hadn't noticed the beauty of the place until Della and Erma came down to get water for camp.

Della stopped when she reached the water's edge and exclaimed, "Look at the reflection of those trees. Aren't they beautiful?" She just stood there staring until the sun went down.

After Della called my attention to it, I could see the water in the lake was so clear it looked like a giant mirror reflecting the blue of the sky and shadows of all the trees, ferns, and flowers along the bank.

Erma had brought a tin cup down with her. Dipping it into the water she said, "I hope this water is as cool as it looks to be. The water in our canteen today became as hot as duck soup."

In the morning, Papa, Walter and Kenneth drove the short distance into Pendleton to see about work. With the men out of the way, Mamma made us carry water from the stream for our baths. She heated it in the old coal-oil can she used for a wash boiler. We all took baths in the washtub before the womenfolks started the wash. Mamma said that she hoped the men could find work here where we had this good supply of water.

In so many of our camps we had to depend on what water we hauled in our canteens. Here the water was handy for camp chores; and we kids enjoyed wading in it, too.

With the water-carrying and the wood-dragging, not to mention the baths we had to take, it was mid afternoon before I was free to look around our new camp.

Mamma made me take Violet and Bud with me. I was thankful when she said that she would keep Chuckles. If I'd had him, I would've had to carry him over all the rough places as we wandered up the stream.

We had gone maybe half a mile upstream, jumping rocks and wading from one bank to the other, when we came upon an old dead cow. She was all swelled up and stinking and had the stream practically dammed up. The water was running around both sides of her and seeping through under her swollen body.

Of course that ended our exploring trip. We had to race back to camp to tell Mamma.

Water

I was in the lead as we came in sight of camp. I was afraid the other kids might break the news first, so I started yelling, "Mamma, there's an old dead cow in our water upstream!"

My hollering started the other kids to begin yelling too, I guess with our jumbled-up voices, Mamma couldn't under-stand anything we were saying, because when we reached camp she said, "Now if you will calm down and tell me what the trouble is and do it one at a time, I might understand.

"Bud was still yelling, "Dead cow! Dead cow!" I told him to shut up and let me tell the story.

When I finished telling what we had found, Mamma exclaimed, "Not in the water we've been drinking! I sure hope none of us get sick. I did think that water had a funny smell when I made my tea at noon. We'll have to

The early thirties; Charley (Chuckles) and Bud one morning, ready for school.

move out of this place as soon as Dad gets back."

The men returned to camp in a couple of hours. Mamma and the girls had almost everything packed and ready to leave. They had even gathered the half-dry clothes and put them into the washtub, planning on re-hanging them when we reached our next camp.

Papa said that it was just as well we moved on anyway. They had spent all day in town looking for work and had even wasted gas driving to a dam site under construction north of Pendleton. Here they were told there were already more men waiting in line than would be hired. However, someone told them that they might get work on a road job south of town. That was where we would head next.

Erma and Walter were the last to leave camp. They hadn't caught up with us when they ran out of gas. They were lucky though, because a few more miles down the road and they would have been stranded in a land with nothing in sight but sand. As it happened they were only a few feet from a small store with a gas pump out front.

Walter searched through his pockets and only found twenty cents. He thought that wasn't enough money to buy any gas. Suddenly a bright idea flashed through his mind. This was such a small store it was worth a try.

He pushed the car up to the gas pump and when the proprietor came out, Walter asked him, "About how much gas do you think it will take to get me out to that road job south of here?"

"Oh, not more than a couple of gallons," was the answer he received. Walter continued talking about the other two cars that were with him and how they expected him to reach the road job before dark. He went into detail, saying one car belonged to his father-in-law and family and the other one was owned by his brother-in-law and wife. He kept the conversation going by asking about the weather up here or anything he could think of until the man had put the two gallons of gas in the tank. He then turned toward the store as though he intended to buy some groceries.

Once inside he casually asked, "I suppose you have change for twenty? That's all I have."

Back in those days a twenty dollar bill was a large sum of money. It was probably worth more than a couple of hundred dollars at today's money value.

The man went over and dragged his cigar box cash register from under the counter and scratching around in the few bills he had in it, he said, "Naw, I don't think I can make the change. You'll probably be coming by here later to buy gro-ceries. You can stop in then and pay the thirty-eight cents you owe me."

When Walter returned to the car Erma asked him how he had paid for the gas with only twenty cents. Walter told her the man said that they could pay later.

"That was nice of him to trust us," she said as they drove off.

When we reached the area where the road job was, we found much the same conditions existed here as we had found back at Wagner. The sand was just as deep and the wind was blowing just as strong. The only difference here was, they would hire men with cars.

The only place we could find to camp was over a mile from the job. We were out of gas and broke as usual, so the men had no choice. They had to go to work although it meant walking a long distance through the sand.

Our men had worked three days, when one exceptionally hot afternoon Kenneth was caught taking a drink of water from the boss's canteen. The fat slob of a boss started cussing Kenneth and told him to bring his own water to the job if he needed to drink.

Papa, who was standing near, decided that was more than any man should have to take from his boss. He walked over to the guy and in no uncertain terms told him, "If you're so tight you can't even furnish water for your men, we'll move on down the road out of this Hell's Hole."

Once more we had to swipe gas to get away from a job. This time the men put gas in one of our good canteens. Mamma never succeeded in washing that canteen well enough to remove the gassy taste from the water. Once in awhile someone would use that canteen to fill the teakettle, and when Mamma made her tea we would all hear about it.

CHAPTER SEVENTEEN

Columbia River Country

As we drew near the Columbia River, the country became rougher. Rolling hills turned into steep mountains. The road, at times, became only a narrow ledge carved out of the mountainside. Sometimes it seemed to be backtracking as it wound into deep canyons and out again.

We were going around a sharp curve that led up a steep grade when our car, which was in the lead, sputtered a few times, then died.

Back in the twenties this road along the Columbia River was considered a first class highway. There was room for two cars to meet or pass anywhere on it. It was nothing like the mountain roads back in Arizona. There if you met a car or wanted to pass one, the nearest turnout, made especially for that purpose, had to be found by one of the drivers. Here with our three cars parked on the road there was room for another car to pass, but absolutely no room left over for a woman to herd a bunch of wild kids like we were.

At first Mamma tried to make us all sit in the back of the truck. That didn't last long, because as I tried to stretch my cramped leg I accidently kicked Violet. She wasn't hurt, but she reached out and scratched my bare leg below my knee pants. She almost brought the blood, too. To get even, I kicked her so hard she started bawling and rolled over onto Bud, and he started to cry.

Mamma told me to get out of the car and try to behave myself. I thought I was obeying her when I walked over to the side of the road to see how far it was to the bottom of the canyon. Before I got a good look she yelled, "Laura! Get away from that bank before you fall over it."

Then Violet began to complain, "I don't see why Bud and I have to stay in the car when you let Laura get out and do whatever she wants to."

Mamma could see the struggle she would have if she had to keep us here much longer. She said to Papa, "I might as well take the things I'll need to fix dinner. I'll get Walter to take the little kids, the food, and me on up the road. Maybe we'll be able to find a wider spot to park and I can cook dinner."

After loading the kids, Mamma squeezed her body into the already overloaded cab of Walter's little coupe. Sticking her head out the side opening she said, "Virgie, there ain't room for you and Laura. You can walk on up the road until Dad and Kenneth get our car started and catch up with you. Laura, you keep away from those high bluffs. Do you hear?"

Virgie and I had topped the first hill on our hike and were sitting on a rock beside the road getting our breath back, when a big, fancy two-seated black car pulled up beside us and stopped. The driver stuck his head out the window and asked, "Would you girls like to ride?"

He sure was a classy-looking dude. His black hair

was slicked back with some kind of grease and his pretty tie looked nice against his white shirt.

He must have felt sorry for us walking up all those steep curves; why else would a guy like that want to pick up a couple of country hicks? I know neither of us had used a comb or washed our faces since early morning, and riding in the back of an open truck with the wind blowing dust in our faces didn't improve our appearance.

I don't remember what Virgie was wearing, but I know I had on the coveralls Della had brought up from Jerome when we were camped at Stoneman Lake in Arizona. I was always rough on my clothes and the coveralls were the only outer garments I had left. By now these coveralls were really out-standing, because the lower end of the legs reached only a little below my knees. This left several inches of my bare legs exposed before they entered the tops of an old pair of men's high-top work shoes. These shoes Kenneth had found in a culvert in Idaho, and as I had no shoes he gave them to me. They almost fit my feet. I was so mad I threw them behind a bush. It was bad enough to wear old Boy Scout shoes, but to think he expected me to wear any body's old cast-off shoes was too much. When I threw them away, Violet happened to be looking and ran and told Mamma what I had done. Mamma made me go get them. She said to me, "Don't be silly. We hardly have enough money for food. If we get in a snowstorm before we get back to Arizona, you'll be thankful to have any kind of shoes on your feet."

Our parents always bought each of us a pair of Boy Scout shoes just before school started in the fall. These shoes lasted until school was out in the spring. That is, they lasted with a lot of Papa's cobbler work holding them together. Papa would resole our shoes, sew them up when they ripped, and even sew patches on the uppers if they needed it.

The other kids were never as hard on their shoes as I

was. My shoes were always ready to fall apart by the time school was out. This year was no exception. I had gone barefoot all summer, but now with cold weather, Mamma made me wear those hated, old, men's shoes.

We must have been a strange looking pair to the driver of that big city car as we stood up when he spoke to us. He climbed out and opened the back door. He probably thought if we sat too close to him we might give him fleas or something.

That was all right with us, we thought, as we climbed into the roomy back seat and sat on the shiny soft black leather cushion. He slammed the door, walked around to the front of the car, got in the driver's seat and we were off.

We began pretending we were really high-class, holding our backs straight and our heads up high. We were making believe we were rich ladies and the driver was our chauffeur. The big letdown came when we discovered our chauffeur was watching every move we made in a big mirror up front. We had never ridden in a car with a rear-view mirror. During the rest of our ride we hunched down in the corner of the seat, like two embarrassed schoolgirls caught unexpectedly making eyes at their good-looking math teacher.

When we reached the little glen where Walter's car was parked, we thanked the man and quickly climbed out of his car. As we rushed over to where Erma and Mamma were busy with the lunch chores as he drove off, I was thinking, *I'll bet that character will never forget the two strange-looking girls he picked up on that mountain road.*

Somewhere back up the road Mamma had bought a hard rind winter squash from a vegetable stand beside the road. She had half a Dutch oven of it fried for our lunch, and did it smell good. I could hardly wait until I could sample it.

When Kenneth's car, pulling Papa's car, came into

Columbia River Country

sight and ground to a stop beside our campfire, Mamma set the graniteware plates out and said to get washed up for dinner. I was already washed, so I grabbed my plate and headed for the squash. I took a good half of it into my plate. I had taken it just in time, because Kenneth came along and took the other half. Noone said anything to Kenneth, but as soon as Mamma saw my heaped-up plate she said, "Laura, don't you know there's ten other hungry people? You march right back over to the Dutch oven and put most of that squash back."

I was mad. I put back most of the squash, but I couldn't see why Kenneth could keep all he had taken. It just never occurred to me, the rest of the family might like to have a little squash to go along with their beans.

Some of the most beautiful country we saw on the whole trip was along the Columbia River. Coming from Arizona where the streams we had seen were small, we gazed with awe at this great, roaring, tumbling river. It was even bigger than Oak Creek during a flood stage. Farther on in Oregon we crossed many streams that reminded us of our own beautiful Oak Creek, but this river was like thousands, maybe millions of little Oak Creeks put together and rushing to the Pacific Ocean.

The Columbia River forms the boundary between Oregon and Washington. Up to this time we could count seven states we had visited. They were Arizona, New Mexico, Colorado, Utah, Nevada, Idaho, and Oregon. If we could have crossed that big river we could have bragged about being in Washington. We saw one bridge across the river, but it was a toll bridge, and of course we didn't have money for anything as foolish as that. We had to be content just looking across that big river at the state of Washington.

Along the river near The Dalles we saw many salmon factories. Not far from each factory were small Indian villages where the factory workers lived. When we came to the first of these villages, we saw something hanging on lines near each hut. At first we thought it was hunks of meat hanging there to dry into jerky. We soon learned, after a closer look and by the smell, it was fish. After that we could always tell by the terrible fishy odor when we were getting close to one of these villages.

The road passed through several tunnels as we drove along beside the river. One was quite long and had large windows on the riverside. We drove into the parking area by one of these windows and looked down at that big river directly below us. Papa said the windows were built to let light into the tunnel, as well as allowing the tunnel builders to dump the dirt and rocks into the river rather than hauling them the long distance to the entrance.

It was somewhere along the Columbia River that we lost the pinchers. I suppose only a few people today would have any idea what a valuable tool the pinchers were. I don't know if all families in our day had pinchers, but in our family the only tools Papa had were a saw, a hammer and the pinchers.

As far back as I can remember, there was never a house built, a fence put up, a big or little wagon fixed, a set of stilts made, or a pair of shoes soled, without the help of the pinchers. They were used to drive nails, cut wire or tin, and the handles were used for prying. I guess they must have been used for fixing flat tires too, because that was what they were being used for the day they were lost.

I had heard Papa say many times, "You kids have lost my pinchers." This time they were lost forever, because we were miles away before we discovered they'd been left behind.

Losing the pinchers was a tragedy for the entire family and a loss that was not replaced. As far as I can remember, we never got another pair of pinchers.

CHAPTER EIGHTEEN

Among the Apple Farmers

After many months of travel we at last reached our destination, Hood River, Oregon. This was the place where we had planned on making so much money we could travel the rest of the way home without having to stop and look for work. I even thought we might have enough money to buy some badly-needed clothes, and still have money left so we could get off our skimpy diet.

I was surprised to find the campgrounds here looked much the same as the ones we had been staying in all along the trip. There was the usual unpainted two-holer, with a piece of bailing wire nailed to the door. When you wished to lock the door, the wire was wrapped around a nail that had been driven into the inside door casing. Nearby was the same kind of old pit where we were to throw our garbage. Even the people here didn't look as prosperous as I thought they would. Their clothes were covered with as many patches as ours. I really don't know what I expected, but I know I was disappointed.

I remember one unusual character that joined our campfire gang the first night we were here. He was one of those guys who could talk all night if he had a listening audience.

He was telling some big yarn to the menfolks, when he heard Mamma say to Della, "I don't mind traveling, but I wish I had some easy way to keep the kids' heads clean. It seems every time we stop for a few days I spend half the time carrying water, heating it, then going through the unpleasant task of washing kids' heads. It was hard enough at home where I had a decent place to work. In camp, trying to poke their heads into a washtub on the ground is a back-breaking job."

That guy was engrossed in his big yarn, but somehow he heard Mamma mention head-washing. That was all it took to make him quit his big story in order to give Mamma some un-asked-for advice.

"Why wash their hair?" he asked. "I have a son that washed his hair every week, now his head is as slick as an apple. Not a hair left. Now look at the head of hair I have." He bent his head forward and shook it for all to see. I thought it looked like a matted rag-mop. "I never wash my hair," he continued. "Once a month I beat up an egg and rub it into my scalp."

We believed he was telling the truth in that story, because his hair sure looked as if it had never been washed, or combed either. Mamma didn't take his advice. She continued to wash our hair as usual, and as far as the egg was concerned, she thought it better to put it in our bellies and not waste it on our heads.

While we were here, we saw what could have been the forerunner of today's house-cars. It belonged to a rich widow who was just passing through on her way to southern California. She had a one-room house built on the back of a flat-bed truck. We never had the chance to see the inside of the house, but the busybody of this campground did. We found there's always someone in every campground who greets all the new arrivals and finds out all he can about them, so he can tell the other campers. In this camp he happened to be Mr. "Dirty

Head" (that's the name we kids gave to the man that wouldn't wash his head). He told us the inside of the building looked just like a house. There was a bed, a wood-stove and a cupboard with a let-down door that made a table, just like a chuck-box table. There were even two windows with lace curtains, which we could see from the outside. The woman had a hired man to do her driving. He slept in a tent he pitched beside the truck.

We were camped in this campground several days before we found an apple farmer who would hire all of us. We had brought camp cooking equipment for only one camp kitchen, so we all had to be together.

We all worked on this job: some picking from the trees and others collecting the apples that fell on the ground. Violet and Bud helped with the groundwork, but I was considered old enough to help in the trees, if a grown-up was working close by to keep me on the job.

Our picking bags were much the same as the ones we used when we picked prunes. Here we didn't have to be so careful about squashing the apples, and we all liked our boss, Mr. Evans. He never complained about the way we picked his fruit. He paid us by the box, and this gave the women-folks a chance to go to camp early and fix our meals and do the camp chores.

While we were working in his orchards, Mr. Evans allowed us to use a small shed for our kitchen. The big wood cook-stove in one corner really caught Mamma's eyes. After cooking so many meals in the Dutch ovens, she was happy to find he would let her use the stove.

"If I can find a pan to bake it in, we can have a cake for Violet's birthday," Mamma said. Violet's birthday was the twenty-fifth of September, the day after we moved to the apple orchard.

Mamma located a big, square roasting pan behind the cooking shed. It was filled with rusty nails. Mamma dumped the nails out and scrubbed and scoured the pan with ashes, until she considered it clean enough to bake the cake. It was a mighty big cake, and it was good. After going so many months without any decent sweets, we gobbled up that cake at one meal.

When we moved on, Mamma asked Mr. Evans if he wanted the old roast pan. He said no, so we brought it home with us. For years I remember Mamma using that pan to bake her loaves of bread. It was big enough to hold four large loaves of bread. The pan also made many trips to our family picnics when a big cake was needed.

One day Papa was picking on the same tree with me and I was whistling a merry tune in a loud, shrill manner. After awhile Papa asked, "Can't you pick apples without letting out that terrible racket?" I was highly insulted. I couldn't see how my whistling could bother him; in fact I thought he should be enjoying it.

Papa and I were a lot alike. We both could never work long before we either started to whistle or sing. The big difference was Papa carried on in a soft, gentle manner for his own enjoyment, and I thought I was doing everybody a favor by entertaining them.

I quit whistling and kept quiet, because I knew in a short time I could get even with Papa for the smart thing he had said to me. I didn't have long to wait before Papa began one of his tuneless whistles. "I thought you didn't like whistling," I said.

"My whistling isn't near as nerve-racking as that shrill whistle of yours," he replied. Papa quit whistling. I felt terrible, because now neither of us could have music while we worked.

After a few weeks we had picked all the apples, except a few uncolored ones on the lower limbs. Now all we had left was to go back over the orchard and strip the trees.

At lunch one day the grown-ups were discussing whether to look for more apple work or just move on. We had made quite a large sum of money on this job, because we had all worked. All of us together probably had at least a hundred dollars.

Papa said, "By working late tonight I think we can wind this job up by tomorrow evening. What do you

Among the Apple Farmers

think, Mother? It's up to you. If you want to move on toward home, we will."

"I would sure like to get out of here before the fall rains set in. I've been told that once they begin, we can expect rain everyday. That would be a mess to travel in," Mamma answered.

We all agreed with Mamma and planned to break camp and move on down the road when we finished up here, probably day after tomorrow. However, our plans changed. When we reached the orchard, our boss was waiting with a friend.

Mr. Evans' greeting to Papa was, "Mr. Purtymun, I want you to meet a friend of mine, Mr. Sampson. He has a packing shed on the other side of town and would like to hire a couple of you to help him, when you finish up here."

"Glad to meet you," Papa said, while shaking the man's hand. "We were just discussing our plans during our lunch period today, and we sort of thought it would be a good idea to move farther south out of this damp climate before the rains begin. I think we can finish your orchards by tomorrow night," continued Papa. "That would put us on the road day after tomorrow morning. We'd like to stay and help you out, Mr. Sampson, but we've found it doesn't pay for all of us to stay in a spot when only two of us are working."

"Well now," Mr. Sampson cut in, "I'm sure we could fix that up if you stay. I have a neighbor who is behind on his picking and would probably be glad to hire the rest of you. He has some small shacks he lets his pickers live in. They are just across the field from my packing shed."

Soon the rest of our gang returned to the orchard and Papa introduced Mr. Sampson and explained the situation to the grown-ups. "It is up to the majority to decide if we stay, but I was thinking it might be smart to stay here until we could get some sort of roofs built on Kenneth's and my car."

"That's a good idea," Mamma agreed. "With winter coming on and a lot more mountains to cross before we get home, we could sure use some kind of cover over us and our stuff."

"I think we might as well take the jobs, don't you, Hon?" Kenneth said as he turned to get Della's opinion.

"Yes, that'll be all right with me," Della replied.

Walter, as usual, was silent until everyone else had had their say; then in his slow way he began, "Now that summer is over, we might have trouble finding work. We had better work while we have the chance."

"I think so too," Erma said.

So it was decided we would move over to the other orchards and work as long as the jobs held out.

It was getting late in the evening when we left the one farm to move to the other. On the way we stopped at a grocery store to pick up a few items. When we left the store and started down a narrow country road to our new job, it was almost dark. As we drove over a little rise in the road, we all noticed some lights flash down the road a short distance. We didn't have time to figure what it was all about, when something smashed into the front of our car. The next thing we knew, Virgie, Violet, Bud and I and the groceries were all mixed up in the front seat along with Mamma, Papa and Chuckles.

While Mamma was unscrambling all of us and checking to see if anyone was hurt, a young kid showed up on Papa's side of the car. He grabbed Papa by the sleeve and said in a smart-sounding voice, "It's all your fault! Driving without lights! Give me your name and license number, and also where I can get in touch with you. You're sure going to have to pay for this."

Everything had happened so quickly, Papa hadn't had time to get his thoughts together; so he said, "Yes, I guess it was my fault." Then he gave the kid the information he had asked for. Not one word was said about why the lights on the kid's car popped on then off again. The kid didn't even ask if any of us were hurt. He disen-

Among the Apple Farmers

tangled his strip-down from the front of our car, and finding it still ran, he was gone be-fore Kenneth and Walter arrived on the scene.

When Mamma found out none of us were hurt, she asked Walter to take her and the little kids on to the farm where we were to work, leaving Kenneth, Della, Virgie and me to help Papa with our car.

The accident happened only a short distance from Mr. Reeves' (our new boss) farm. It was only a few minutes before Walter was back, riding in Mr. Reeves' car. They had come back to help get Papa's car over to the farm, but they were too late. We already had the wreck tied behind Kenneth's car and were ready to move on.

When Mr. Reeves found he wouldn't be of any help, he said he would go on home. Walter decided to stay with our men, so Mr. Reeves asked Virgie and me to ride back with him.

We had just climbed into the car and were starting off when Mr. Reeves said, "I guess Mr. Sampson picked the best workers for himself."

Virgie became so mad she answered him by saying, "There's no best among us, one of us is as bad as the others."

I have no idea what that man thought of that for an answer, because he never said another word the rest of the way. I thought it was a mighty funny way to answer the man, so I made sure to remember what she had said so I could tell the rest of the gang.

Although we worked on this job for several weeks, we never heard a word from that kid that caused our wreck. Someone told us the kid had been in so many wrecks he didn't dare turn us in. That was the reason he was in such a hurry to get away before someone found out who he was.

Our new boss was a Seventh-Day Adventist, who had tried to hire only workers of the same faith. When he failed to find enough Seventh-Day Adventist apple pickers, he wound up with us.

One unusual thing about working for these people was we all had to quit working in the orchard at noon on Friday. The other working families used Friday afternoons preparing for Saturday, their day of rest. They did all their cooking, washing, and shopping, so they didn't have any chores for their Sabbath. I don't think they even made their beds Saturday morning. They devoted the whole day to worshipping. When they weren't in church, they were reading their Bible or praying in their shacks.

Not belonging to any church, we really went to work for ourselves, not only Friday afternoon, but all day Saturday too. We collected our wood and did the many chores we never had time to do during our working days. The mending alone was enough to keep one woman busy. As our clothes wore out, they sometimes had one patch overlapping another. It was while we were living here that Mamma, when sorting through the mending, came upon a pair of Papa's bib overalls. They were covered with patches and every patch had a hole in it. She flung them to one side in disgust. "I'm sick of tearing old patches off and putting new ones on. I refuse to go over that pair again," she exclaimed.

To Della's surprise, Kenneth went over and picked them up and looked them over. "Hon," he said to Della, "I'm sure with a little more mending I can wear them through a couple of more washes."

Della looked up from her mending and with a positive tone to her voice said, "I can tell you one thing, Mr. Greenwell, when Mamma throws a pair of pants away, there's no need of me trying to mend them because they're already past the mending stage."

Kenneth dropped the pants, and without another word got the drink of water he had come after. Then he high-tailed it back to where the men were working on the cars.

Della and Kenneth went to work for Mr. Sampson.

Among the Apple Farmers 103

Della worked part-time on the apple grader and the rest of the time up at the house helping Mrs. Sampson with the housework. Kenneth was asked to do any job that needed doing on the whole farm. Sometimes he worked on the apple grader, but at times he was asked to mend fences, clean out the chicken houses, or do mechanical work on the old truck that was used on the farm.

One day at the house Mrs. Sampson asked Della, "How old is your husband, Della?"

"He was twenty last spring," Della replied.

"Then how old are you?" Della was asked.

"I'm twenty, too," Della answered.

"Oh! You're older than your husband?"

"No. We're the same age. He was twenty in March and I was twenty in May."

Mrs. Sampson still looked confused, but Della decided not to try to explain.

The twins, Kenneth and Carl Greenwell, about eight years old.

"Last night my husband Bob was commenting on what a good worker Kenneth is. He said Kenneth seemed so dependable on any job he was put on. That's something unusual in such a young man. In fact, Bob thought Kenneth was much younger than twenty."

"Oh, Kenneth and his twin brother Carl began working out when they were very young," Della said. "I have heard them talking about working for a dairy that was down in the Jerome Gulch. It was about two miles from where they lived in Jerome, and down a steep mountainside. A man by the name of Paul Tissaw drove the milk wagon and the twins delivered the milk up both sides of the streets as the wagon went along. They not only delivered milk in Jerome, but in Clarkdale, the smelter town for the Jerome mines. I'm sure the twins couldn't have been more than nine or ten at that time, because they were still quite young when their parents moved to a farm on lower Oak Creek, in a small farming settlement named Cornville. Here the twins learned to do any kind of work connected with the farm. Before Kenneth and I were married, Kenneth worked in lumber yards, garages, smelters, and numerous other jobs."

"You are lucky he is able to do so many different types of work, now that you are traveling and working your way as you go."

"Yes, I guess we are all lucky. My Dad and my brother-in-law, Walter, are like Kenneth. They can do a variety of jobs. On many occasions on this trip we were fortunate to have three men who were able to do almost anything."

By the time we had completed our work at the last apple farms, we were pretty well outfitted to travel again. The men had completed the tops for both Papa's and Kenneth's cars, and we had money for gas and oil.

CHAPTER NINETEEN

Stocking Caps and Streetcar Tracks

The morning we were leaving we went to the big General Mercantile Store in Hood River to stock up on groceries before we took off. Mamma decided to buy each of us kids stocking caps, rather than put up with our squalling with the earache. It seems the Purtymun children always had earaches when their ears were exposed to cold air.

I can still see Mamma walking the floor with the smaller children when their ears ached. She would try any home remedy that was suggested to her. She was always pouring into our ears some kind of liquid she had heated in a teaspoon. This was followed with a wad of cotton, which was supposed to prevent the fumes of the medicine from escaping. Sometimes she would have Papa blow hot smoke from his cigarette into our ears, and that would be followed with the wad of cotton. I remember hearing her tell about a trip she made with Della and Erma, when Erma was a baby. They hadn't been on the train long before Erma began to cry and rub her ear. Someone told Mamma urine was good to stop the earache. After trying every way she could think of to stop Erma's crying, she took Della to the bathroom and caught a small amount of her urine in a water cup. She poured this into Erma's ear. I can't remember any miracle recoveries and I doubt if any of these remedies helped, but they made Mamma feel she was doing all she could to stop the pain.

Now back to my story about the stocking caps. Mamma picked dark blue, brown or black caps for all us younger kids. When Della came to buy hers, she picked the most beautiful snow-white cap I had ever seen. I was so envious I didn't hesitate to say, "Why can Della have that pretty cap and the rest of us have to wear these old ugly ones?"

"It isn't my job to keep Della's clothes clean anymore, so she can get any color she wants," I was told.

I thought to myself, I'll be glad when I get big enough to be allowed to do some of the things I want, as Della and Erma can.

After getting our caps, we were allowed to entertain ourselves while the grown-ups bought the groceries. Several times I had wandered past a big barrel filled with nuts, but each time the little kids were so close behind me I didn't dare swipe any. Finally, in desperation I told Violet I thought Mamma was going to buy some sugar candy and if she would take Bud over to Mamma, maybe they could get some. As soon as the kids were out of my way I grabbed a big handful of the nuts and poked them into my pocket. In my haste to get the nuts out of sight, I had forgotten my coat pocket had a hole in it. When the first nut hit the floor I knew what had happened. Each step I took toward the door more nuts rolled out, and by the time I was safe outside not a nut was left in my pocket.

I guess no one in the store had heard me except Virgie. She had seen what had happened and was furious because I had spoiled her plan. She followed me outside and bawled me out. She had picked up an old magazine and was planning on easing it under her coat, but she thought I had attracted so much attention with my nuts, she didn't dare snitch the book.

The fall rains had just begun when we continued our

Stocking Caps and Streetcar Tracks

journey down the Columbia River. Our bedding kept fairly dry during the daytime under our new roofs, but at night when we bedded down, the water from the ground gradually soaked up into our mattresses. The menfolks pulled ferns and put them under our beds, but they didn't seem to help much. Eventually the mattresses became so heavy it took all three of our men to load them in the mornings.

Kenneth and Della were the only ones in our crowd who slept dry. They still slept in their car under their new top.

We had tried to detour around all the big cities, after our experience in Salt Lake City. Papa, our guide, missed Portland, Oregon completely, but when we reached Salem, Oregon he somehow made the wrong turn and we found ourselves in the heart of the city trying to find our way out.

We drove up one street then down another until we wound up on a very narrow street that dead-ended at a sawmill. There were streetcar tracks down the center of the street and we had to straddle them, as there was not enough room on either side.

When Papa discovered his mistake, he tried to turn the old Ford around. I guess the car was as confused as Papa, because it died and left us sitting on top of the streetcar line. Here we were, blocking the street, when a streetcar came out of the mill and headed toward us.

The car was filled with workers who were headed home after a hard day's work in the mill. The conductor stopped the trolley when he saw us on the tracks. He opened the door and climbed out to see what the trouble was. Our men, who were trying to crank our car, were soon surrounded by mill-workers. They had all followed the conductor out of the car and now were staring at us as if we were freaks. We could have looked a little odd to anyone who lived in a town and never knew how to build car-tops and stuff, but that was no excuse for them to being saying silly things like they did. One big, burly, red-headed guy asked, "Why in the world were you headed into the mill?"

Then another tough-looking character said, "If you're out of gas you won't find any up here."

The one remark that really upset Papa was one from a sour-looking fellow who growled, "It looks like the only way to get that thing moved is to call a junk dealer."

That did it. Papa straightened up from his turn at the crank, and looking around at the millworkers he said in a loud, aggravated voice, "Just hold your horses. We'll be out of your way in a few minutes." He turned and headed for his old homemade jack.

I never remember Papa whipping us. He seldom raised his voice, but when he gave orders in that voice, we knew he meant business and we sure toed the mark.

His voice had the same effect on those millworkers. They quieted down and got out of his way. Everybody watched with astonishment as Papa pulled the old jack from its resting place on the side of the truck, and placed the end of the pole under the axle. With very little effort, he had the hind wheel jacked up. This made the engine turn over easier. It seemed as if Walter hardly touched the crank and the motor started.

We were turned around and headed back down the street before the millworkers could get back into their streetcar. We soon found our way out of that town, with the old bus running as though she had caused no trouble at all.

CHAPTER TWENTY

Oregon Passage

So far the rain we had been in was only a drizzle and our new tops kept us dry and warm. If a drop of water tried to find its way through the roof, all we had to do was rub the canvas where the drop appeared, then run our finger down the canvas to the car's edge. The water would follow our finger's path and drop outside. We had to do this with only the first drop. After that the water would go by itself.

We were somewhere south of Salem when the drizzle turned into a downpour, and no amount of rubbing could detour the water. By mid-afternoon our bedding and everything in the cars was soaked.

Mamma turned to Papa and asked, "Don't you think we have enough money to rent a cabin tonight? None of us will get any sleep out in this rain."

"We'll stop at the next bunch of cabins we come to and talk it over with the kids," Papa answered. They were both yelling in order to be heard above the noise of the engine and the drumming of the rain on our roof.

We soon came to a small group of cabins sitting back in a cove and surrounded by dripping trees. When Papa pulled into the place, our other cars followed. It was raining so hard the menfolks raced over to the little store in front of the cabins to talk over the situation.

When Papa came back to our car and hurriedly climbed inside, he said to Mamma, "We really shouldn't use what money we have left for a cabin, but it looks like we have no choice. The man in the store told us that this hard rain had washed the road *out* about two miles farther on, and if this rain continues it's doubtful if the repairmen will get it fixed before morning. It looks like we're stuck here for the night, so we rented the only cabin he had left."

We were all surprised when we saw the size of the cabin. It couldn't have been more than twelve feet square, and most of the floor space was taken up with the one double bed where Mamma and Papa would sleep. The rest of us dragged our mattresses in and placed them on the floor, leaving no walking area. We even poked part of our mattresses under Mamma's bed in order to get as much floor space as possible.

We had to cook our meals in a community kitchen which we shared with all the other cabin guests. We waited until everyone was through with their evening meal before we carried our sleeping blankets into the kitchen. Then we built a roaring fire in the cookstove, and spread blankets around in an attempt to dry them.

It was a good thing our cabin was the last one the man had to rent. We would have been embarrassed if some late- arrival had wanted to use the kitchen and found our blankets draped over all the chairs and tables. Our blankets were hardly warmed through, when Papa made us go to bed. "What water's left in your blankets will turn to steam as soon as you get into bed, and you'll soon be as warm as toast," he said.

"I'm going to dry our bedding if it takes all night," Erma said. We had just fallen asleep, when Erma and Walter woke us up, walking all over us while trying to make their bed in the dark.

At ten o'clock, the man who owned the place had chased them out of the kitchen when he came to lock it up for the night, so their blankets weren't much drier.

We were more cheerful when we awoke in the morning and found the sun was shining. We were glad to get on the road again, to get out of all this wetness.

The washout had been repaired before we reached it, and we were all in the best of spirits when we stopped at Eugene, Oregon for gas and to eat our lunch.

While Papa was busy building the fire with the wood Walter and Kenneth had gathered, the girls were unloading the necessary utensils for cooking lunch. Mamma was getting ready to make some biscuits. She took the lid off the flour can, then hesitated as she looked inside.

"We are out of seasoning for beans and almost out of flour," Mamma said as she poured the required flour into the mixing bowl. Then she added, "If we have enough money to buy a slab of salt pork, we can cook beans tonight and maybe we won't eat so much bread."

"We better save enough money to buy gas to get over that mountain range ahead. I'll check and see how much money we have," Papa said as he pulled his big, long black purse from the pocket of his britches and dumped the contents on the running board of the old Ford. There were several bills and a handful of change. Kenneth and Walter had now joined him.

"I think, according to the map, we have four or five hundred miles of mountainous country ahead of us, isn't that what you figured, Hon?" Kenneth turned to Della to verify his statement.

"Yes, about that far or more," Della stated, as she joined the menfolks.

Papa picked up the bills and ran them through his fingers to get the wrinkles ironed out; then he said, "We have thirty dollars left. With good luck, that ought to be enough for gas, don't you think, Walt?"

"Well, it should be," Walter answered in his slow way. "A slab of salt pork runs around three dollars. Now I'll see how much change we have," Papa said as he picked out the fifty-cent pieces, then the quarters and dimes. "Hey! We've lots of money. There's over four dollars in change."

"Della," Mamma spoke, as she looked in the direction from which we had come. "Why don't you and Kenneth walk back to that store we just passed, and get the salt pork while these biscuits are cooking." She then turned the Dutch oven of biscuits over to Papa to cook.

"I think I'll go with you for the exercise," Virgie spoke up. I quit my game of hopscotch instantly, thinking it might be more fun going to a store than playing with Violet and Bud.

Mamma knew what I was thinking before I said a word, because she ordered me to stay where I was and look after I the kids.

As Della, Kenneth and Virgie started down the street, I muttered low so the grown-ups couldn't hear me, "It ain't fair, it just ain't fair."

Bud heard me and started mimicking me. "Ain't fair! It just ain't fair!" he said.

When I lost control and yelled, "Shut up!" Papa heard me and said, "Laura!" in his tone of voice that meant be quiet. I thought, *Why does everybody have to treat me so mean?*

Upon arriving at the store, the clerk took Kenneth into a storeroom in the back part of the store to get the salt pork. Della and Virgie were wandering around in the store looking at all the goodies they couldn't buy, when the clerk came back alone. Della asked, "Where did my husband go with the salt pork?"

"When he saw the back door," the clerk replied, "your husband asked if it was all right for him to use it instead of coming back through the store. He told me you had the money to pay for the meat."

"Oh," Della said, as she hurriedly dug the money out

of her coat pocket, counted out the change, and handed it to the clerk. When Della and Virgie reached the street, they were surprised to see Kenneth walking up the street with a sack of flour under the slab of salt pork. They ran to catch up with him.

"Where did you get that flour? I only paid for the salt pork," Della asked.

"There was a big stack of flour there, and I remembered Mamma saying we were almost out of flour; so I just picked up the sack of flour along with the salt pork," stated Kenneth.

"Why don't you hurry and get away from the store with it. Don't just stand there. Someone will see you," whispered Della.

"Hell! No one'll know I didn't pay for it. The only one I need to worry about is that store clerk, and from the amount of people going into the store, he'll be too busy to come out to check on me. If I ran down the street everybody would be suspicious."

Kenneth may have felt safe as he ambled down the street, but Della and Virgie sure didn't. They hurried away from Kenneth and walked the rest of the way back to camp on the opposite side of the street.

Upon reaching the higher elevations at Grants Pass, Medford, and Klamath Falls, Oregon, we ran into our first snows.

I don't remember having any serious trouble in the snow. I guess we and our old cars had grown accustomed to accepting any obstacle nature or the human race put in our path. A little snow was nothing for us to get excited about.

The only incident pertaining to the snow that has stuck in my mind all these years happened after we left Klamath Falls. We had probably crossed the state line and were in California. I don't remember the reason we had stopped, but it was probably to cook lunch. It was very cold and we had built a big bonfire of pitch knots to keep ourselves warm. We were there for some time and the smoke from our fire turned the white of Della's beautiful cap into the most horrible blackish color. I took my navy blue cap off my head and looked at it; it was only a little darker and didn't look bad at all. I couldn't keep my mouth shut. I called everybody's attention to her cap by saying, "Aren't you sorry now that you bought that old white cap? You should have been smart like the rest of us and bought a dark one." Della couldn't think of anything to say to me, so she just gave me a dirty look.

The family years later at Mamma and Papa's fiftieth wedding anniversary. Back row: Virgie Russell, Albert Purtymun, Erma Baker, Clara Purtymun, Bud Purtymun, Della Greenwell. Front row: Laura McBride, Zola Hernandez, Violet Rupe.

CHAPTER TWENTY-ONE

Wintering in Cottonwood

Our road wound down out of the high mountains into a big valley, which was probably the upper end of the great Sacramento Valley. As we continued to head south, we eventually crossed the Sacramento River.

Not long after we hit this valley we noticed a very tall peak in the distance. It seemed to be on fire because we saw wisps of smoke rising from its top. Before anyone had a chance to say a word about it, Virgie announced, "We are looking at the only live volcano in the United States." The rest of the bunch thought she was smart to know something like that. I couldn't see it was so important; just an old mountain on fire.

Our next stop was at Cottonwood, California. We found a camping spot on the bank of a small stream under some enormous oak trees. The ground was covered with the biggest acorns I had ever seen. In Arizona there are several kinds of oak trees, but the trees and the acorns are much smaller. During the late summer when the Blackjack acorns begin to fall, I had spent many pleasant hours under the trees eating the acorns. Of course, one could never expect to get a full stomach on the nuts as they were quite small, and most of the time when the shell was parted, one would find a worm had already eaten half the goodies. I cracked one of these big acorns hoping to find good eating inside. What a disappointment. It wasn't fit to eat.

The menfolks went into town to look for work. They were back shortly with good news. They had found a wood-cutting job six miles out of Cottonwood in a large oak woods. Without delay we loaded our stuff and were soon at our new campsite. There were already several woodcutters camped there when we arrived; all were men without families. The only woodcutters I remember were a couple of black men who were very nice to us.

The men cut down the trees and chopped the wood into cookstove lengths. Mamma and we kids stacked the wood in a pile four feet wide by four feet high and eight feet long. This pile of wood was called a cord, and we were paid so much per cord. It couldn't have been very much because we were still poor.

We did manage to buy a big fourteen by fourteen foot army tent to live in. With winter here, it was getting mighty cold and sometimes wet to have to live without any shelter at all. Our tent was one of those teepee-type tents, with a. pole in the middle to hold it up.

We had that tent for years after we got back to Arizona. Quite often when Papa was working on road jobs, we continued to live in it. We always referred to it as our circus tent.

Erma and Walter bought a small tent and a little sheet-iron cookstove with an oven and moved off to themselves while we were here. Della and Virgie resented this because Walter kept his money and spent it for things for himself and Erma, instead of putting it into the family fund as Kenneth did.

Wintering in Cottonwood

Erma always loved to bake cookies, cakes, puddings, and other goodies. While she was living with our big mob she wasn't allowed to do much fancy cooking. After she moved into her own tent, quite often she would bake some nice tidbits and bring a small portion over to us. This would upset Della and Virgie to no end.

One day, after leaving some cookies, she heard a remark before she was out of earshot. She wasn't sure who the speaker was, but the remark, "I guess the queen is feeling sorry for us again," was definitely meant for her.

She came back and eavesdropped near the tent, and there she heard many things that were anything but complimentary. When she could stand no more of the talk, she began to cry and started to run back to her tent. As she rounded the corner of our tent she met Mamma. There were tears streaming down Erma's face and Mamma knew someone had hurt her feelings. When Mamma couldn't get anything out of Erma, she went into our tent; seeing the cookies and Della and Virgie sitting there looking guilty, she soon straightened them out.

We were told by one of the woodcutters that the man who owned the woods would pay seventy cents a sack for all the acorns we picked up. He had some pigs and was fattening them on the acorns.

If we could get ahead on the wood stacking, Mamma and we girls would pick up acorns. We worked hard every spare minute we had, and finally gathered ten or more gunny-sacks full. Then we discovered the man had decided to turn the pigs loose and let them do their own picking. What a disappointment, after all the work it took to pick up those acorns.

I'm glad that man didn't hear the nasty things we said about him as we dumped the acorns on the ground and watched the pigs eat them. He probably would have sent us all to prison for the slanderous things we said.

We had a little more time to pursue our own desires

now that the acorn business had failed. One day while Della was looking through the *Fancy Needlework Book,* she found a pattern telling how to make ladies' purses out of old inner tubes. She asked the rest of us to join her in starting a small purse factory, providing we could talk the men out of a few old tubes.

She said, "If we couldn't make money picking up acorns, we might as well try something else." We had so many old patched tubes the men were willing to part with a few, so we started right into our purse-making.

When I was trying to remember just how those purses looked so I could describe them, a sudden thought came to me. Hadn't I seen my old rubber purse somewhere stowed away in one of my old boxes or trunks of junk?

We have lived in this one spot for forty years and through the years we have built several shacks on our property for one purpose or another. Each shack has gradually been filled to the overflowing state with things we no longer used but thought someday might come in handy.

I thought I would try the chicken house first, because I knew a couple of old cowhide trunks were stored there. This particular shack has no floor, only the earth; there are no windows, and the roof is covered with panels of sheet-iron that had been used many times on previous buildings. During our wet seasons the rain had seeped through the many nail holes of the roof and under the side walls, giving the whole place a musky smell. When I first entered the building, I had to pause for a few minutes so my eyes would grow accustomed to the darkness. I pushed my way around a discarded old-fashioned washing machine, stepped over a big roll of worn-out rug, and on past several boxes and lard cans filled with odds and ends, before I could reach the trunks.

The first and smaller trunk contained a variety of

Wintering in Cottonwood

Christmas decorations. They were all beyond using, but I had kept them for sentimental reasons. When I raised the lid of the bigger trunk I was greeted by a moldy smell. I soon found myself digging through old coats and bathing suits, neat bundles of scrap material I had saved for patches or making quilts. There were boxes of old letters and Christmas cards, and a lot of stuff that had no value but I thought I might need sometime. Sure enough, on the very bottom of the trunk I found my purse.

It was sort of moldy and, due to heat from many Arizona summers, it had melted and the two sides were stuck together. It was so brittle I didn't dare try to pull it apart or it would have crumbled.

In spite of the way it had been treated for the fifty-odd years, I could see it must have been a nice-looking purse when it was first made.

As I look at my old purse I can see the first thing we had to do was split the tubes the long way around. The next problem was to find, without patches, two pieces of tube big enough to cut both sides and the handles of a purse out of. I remember one of the patterns was square and another one was oblong. The purse I made was rounded on the bottom edge. Della and Erma had embroidery thread, so we worked blanket-stitching or French knots around the edge to hold the two pieces together. On the sides we embroidered flowers or something. I can see mine has butterflies and flowers. We even made fringe on some of them by back-stitching an inch or so in from the edge, then cutting the rubber outside the back-stitching to form the fringe.

Our purses looked so nice when they were finished, we were sure with Christmas coming up someone would want to buy them for presents.

About once a week some of us would walk the six miles into Cottonwood to get the mail and pick up any small items that were needed, so we could get by until one of the men could take time off from their woodcutting to drive a car into town for our staple groceries. We decided, on the next trip into town, we would take some of our purses and try to sell them.

Erma and Virgie had chosen to make the trip, but when I found out they were taking the purses, I decided I would go along too. At first Mamma said no, I would have to stay home and help her. After a little begging she softened and said I could go. Then Violet, thinking she had to go everywhere I went, began to whine and beg.

Della, who was drying the dishes, placed the cup she was drying in the dish-box and turned around and said to Mamma, "Why don't you let them both go? All they do around here is fight. I'll help you until they get back."

We were all filled with excitement as we headed for town that sunshiny morning. All I could think of was the money I would have after I sold my purse.

We reached the post office and picked up the mail with no mishap. Then we started down the street in search of a place to try our salesmanship. We had only gone a short distance when a group of boys following us started yelling, "I see London, I see France; I see someone's underpants!" If they had come closer and taken a good look at what they thought were Erma's underpants, they would have discovered it was only an orange-colored patch on her outer britches.

Those boys upset us and we immediately lost our enthusiasm and excitement about the plan. When we did get into a likely-looking shop, we were embarrassed and were each trying to push someone else up front to do the talking. I guess the proprietor thought we were trying to sell stolen goods, because he told us he wasn't interested in our purses and he refused to look at our treasures.

That was the only shop we tried, because we were so up-set all we wanted was to get out of that awful town before something dreadful happened to us.

On the way home from our purse-selling trip, we took a shortcut through the woods. We were walking along the bank of a big canal that was dry except in low places, where there was water for a few hundred feet. We kept noticing a movement in the water, causing it to splash and become muddy. When we crawled down the bank for a closer look we discovered there were fish in the pond.

We couldn't sell purses, but we decided we would try our luck at fishing. Having no fishing equipment, we had to concoct some method of catching fish with whatever we could find handy. Someone suggested we run the fish up and down in their small swimming pool until they were tired, then we might be able to get them out of the water some way.

We picked up sticks from the nearby woods and the race began. Every time the fish stopped to rest we would poke them. If one of us gave out another one of us took her place. Those poor fish didn't have a chance when they got mixed up with the Purtymun clan.

During one of my turns of rest a bright thought hit me. We had just crawled through an old dilapidated fence, and I thought surely I could find a piece of wire on it and use it to "rope" a fish.

I jumped up from where I was sprawled on the bank of the pond and rushed back to the fence. There was a lot of wire all right, but most of it was still tied to the posts. I found a couple of posts that were lying on the ground, and by putting a rock under the wire and pounding it with another rock, I managed to break off a piece. I now had a wire about fifteen feet long to use as a lasso.

We still had a lot of running to do before we had those fish worn down to where we could tie the wire around one of their heads tight enough to pull the fish out of the water, but we finally succeeded.

Our next problem was how were we going to carry

the center of a long pole, and by two of us big girls putting the ends of the pole on our shoulders we started for home. Even then the fish's tail dragged on the ground. We had picked the smallest fish to catch because the bigger ones had sores on their backs. We figured the sun had blistered them where they stuck out of the shallow water.

Our fish turned out to be a salmon, which had probably come up the Sacramento River to spawn. I don't know why they were in the canal when the water was turned out, but I do know we really enjoyed the fish diet we went on for several days. We had salmon patties, salmon steaks, salmon loaves, and baked salmon, to name a few choice dishes we made out of that big fish. It was quite a change from our regular meatless diet.

CHAPTER TWENTY-TWO

Christmas

For the past months Chuckles, our baby, had been waking up crying after he had gone to sleep at night. Although his eyes were open, he didn't seem to recognize any of us. At times it would be an hour or so before Mamma could get him settled down and back to sleep. Until recently these spells had been attacking him only a few times a month. Suddenly they were occurring every night, and seemed to last longer with each one he had.

It was almost Christmas time, but we were all so worried about Chuckles that the thought of a Christmas celebration never entered our heads. We decided to hold a family consultation to find the best way to combat our new problem. We had very little money, and knew nothing about the doctors in Cottonwood. It was decided that Mamma would write to Grandma Cook, Papa's mother, and ask for enough money for the train fare. Then Mamma and Chuckles would go to Fresno where Grandma Cook and Papa's two sisters lived. Papa's sisters were both nurses, and we figured they probably knew a good doctor who would examine the baby. They were living in the city too, where hospitals and medical help were available. We thought Chuckles would have better care there than we could give him in our tent.

We were all hoping that nothing serious was wrong with Chuckles. If that were so, we could stay working at the wood job until we made a little more money, and then we could drive the four hundred miles on down to Fresno.

We were all very sad when we put Mamma and Chuckles on that train to go to Fresno. Mamma had never been separated from her family for any length of time. She had tears in her eyes as she kissed us goodbye. We could see her waving from the window as long as she could see us standing on the station platform.

Although we missed Mamma and Chuckles a lot, we managed to have a fairly nice Christmas without them. The little Christmas tree we had cut looked pretty standing in the corner of our tent, all decorated with strings of popcorn and colored paper chains. Before we went to bed Christmas Eve we even sang a few Christmas carols.

Erma and Della made each of us a nice handkerchief out of floursack material. They were hem-stitched around the edges and had embroidered flowers in the corner. The handkerchiefs looked so nice I thought it would be a shame to blow our noses on them. I did think we could put them in our pockets and show them to people, though.

Papa bought some nuts and hard candy and even let the girls buy a small roast and some sweet potatoes to cook for Christmas dinner. Erma made a big cobbler and opened some canned string beans and brought them over when she and Walter joined our dinner party.

I doubt if even wealthy people had a better feast than ours.

One of the colored woodcutters came over and wished us a Merry Christmas, and gave each of us a Christmas card he had made. They were just small pieces of unlined tablet paper with a picture of flowers or something drawn on them. Mine had a rose branch with three roses on it and under the drawing was a little note. This is what was written on mine: "Wisher 1925, put me in a wire wing in the bank."

The cards didn't make much sense to us, but the pictures were pretty and the man could sure write neat. We thought he was mighty nice to spend so much time trying to help us have a good Christmas.

I still have my slip of paper after fifty-three years have passed. I look at it occasionally and still admire the drawings, but don't understand the message any better now than I did when it was given to me.

A few days after Christmas we received a letter from Mamma. In it she stated that the doctor could find nothing seriously wrong with Chuckles, and his problem was only nightmares. Mamma also told us in the letter that Chuckles had had only one bad spell after they arrived in Fresno.

Although the letter was a little late, its message was the best present we had received for Christmas. We had all tried to be jolly during the holidays, but we were worried about our baby and we missed Mamma.

The Doctor was right when he diagnosed Chuckle's ailment as nightmares, because he continued having these spells after he was grown.

One night, many years after we returned home, Charley (we dropped the nickname of Chuckles when we grew older) was sleeping out in our orchard in Oak Creek Canyon. It was summertime and we kids always slept outside as soon as the weather warmed up. Charley had a nightmare in which he and his little sister Zola and his niece Dorothy (Erma's baby) were playing in the middle of the road. He dreamed he heard a big truck coming and he yelled, "Run, kids, run!" He jumped out of bed and ran. He woke up when he hit a fruit tree and fell to the ground. It was several weeks before his face healed from the skinning and bruises he'd received when he hit that tree.

Another time after I was married, a close friend of Charley's who was visiting with him at the time told this story about one of Charley's nightmares. Charley was in his late teens when this happened. Our parents were living on a ranch south of Sedona, but still on Oak Creek. It was much warmer down there than it was at our usual habitats up in the Canyon, so the whole family was sleeping outside.

The beds were scattered over most of the yard. In the bright moonlight Papa heard some jibbering going on in the direction of Charley's bed. He could easily see Charley's sheet-draped figure running toward a barbed-wire fence. Papa didn't take time to untangle himself from his bedding. He hit the ground running and dragged his sheet with him. He knew he had to catch the boy before Charley would tear himself to pieces on the barbed wire. They ran in the direction where they had staked a calf. These two sheet-covered running creatures frightened the calf, and he ran with such force to the end of his chain that he pulled the tether stake out of the ground. The calf then, with his chain and stake flying through the air, led the stampede.

To an uninformed observer, these figures chasing each other in the middle of the night must have been a startling sight.

The race ended when Charley became so entangled in his sheet that he toppled to the ground, where Papa fell on top of him. Luckily, not even the calf reached the fence, because it turned in time to avoid the barbed wire by making a mad dash toward the barn. Everyone was wide-awake by time Charley and Papa returned to bed after re-staking the calf. It was hours before there was any more sleep that night.

Mamma (Clara Purtymun) and son Charley, in his teens, pose for a snapshot. (Charley's 8th grade graduation day; taken in front of the schoolhouse which stood across the creek from Slide Rock.)

CHAPTER TWENTY-THREE

Yard-Camped at Grandma Cook's

By the end of January we had saved enough money to take us on to Fresno. On the day we were leaving, we rose before daylight and had the tents down and everything loaded by the time it was light enough to see how to drive. We planned on reaching Fresno in about a week. Four miles out of Cottonwood our old car broke down and we wasted the whole day working on it.

After that first day of trouble, we rolled merrily along and arrived in Fresno late in the evening on the seventh day.

Aunt Ida and her husband Bob owned several acres of land on the edge of town. They let us pitch our tent in their yard. Uncle Bob had been trying to find someone to plow his garden plot, so he was glad to pay Papa to do the work.

We were all happy to get Mamma and Chuckles back into our big tent. The big girls were all right for awhile, but they never seemed to get the chores done like Mamma did. She always had the biscuits cooked on time and

Yard-Camped at Grandma Cook's

I never had to worry about making my bed before I crawled into it. I don't know how she did it, but everything began to run smooth again when Mamma took over.

Grandma Cook lived in a small house surrounded by fruit and shade trees. She always had to have her fruit trees wherever she lived. She had raised a big family, six boys and two girls, on farms where they grew most of their own food. After so many years of canning so they would have food to last through the winter, it was hard for Grandma to quit preparing for the lean time of the year. She gave most of the fresh fruit away, but she still canned enough to keep both her daughters supplied with jams, jellies, and home-canned fruit.

When Grandma was younger she did all her pruning and other work in caring for the trees. Now her daughters thought she was getting too old to climb the trees and ladders, so she hired someone to do that type of work. She was glad to hire Walter and Kenneth when she found out they could prune trees.

When we arrived, Grandma was in the middle of her yearly housecleaning. This was the time of the year when she emptied all her cupboards, washed all the unused dishes, and washed or painted the inside of her kitchen.

I think Grandma knew how poor we were, because she hired Della to help with this cleaning.

One evening just before quitting time, Kenneth came to Grandma's back door and asked, "Grandma, we have finished all the trees in the back of your house. Don't you think it would be better to wait until morning to start the pruning in your front yard? Someone might want to use the front door, and they would break their necks in the dark if there were limbs all over the place."

"That's a good idea, Kenneth," Grandma said. She and Della had all of Grandma's best dishes and china stacked on the kitchen table. Della was washing and

Grandma was drying and replacing each piece in the freshly-scrubbed china closet.

"Kenneth, if you go home now, you'll have to come back after me in a couple of hours. I can't leave Grandma with these dishes scattered all over the place," Della explained. "Grandma can't even make a cup of tea in this mess "

"Oh, that'll be all right, Della," Grandma said. "Ida said she was going shopping with a friend. I asked her to pick up a few things for me. She'll be coming by here later and you can ride home with her."

Aunt Ida had never learned to drive a car. She usually caught a streetcar to get where she wanted to go. Today she rode the streetcar downtown, but was supposed to meet a friend who would drive her back home.

It was late when Aunt Ida and her friend came by for Della. Della was tired from scrubbing cupboards and walls all day, and she was nervous, having had to wash all of Grandma's fancy dishes. She had to be careful so she wouldn't chip or break them; after all, it was quite a change from scrubbing our old graniteware stuff.

As I look back on it, I can see now why Della was so upset when they drove into the yard not far from our tents, and Aunt Ida's friend asked sarcastically, "Ida, do you have gypsies camped in your yard?"

Della climbed out of the car and without even a "thank you" came bustling over to our tent.

As she rushed away from the car she heard Aunt Ida say in a calm voice, "Oh, no! That's only my brother and his family. They've been traveling."

Aunt Ida was that way. It seemed nothing people said or thought of her could upset her. I will always remember one of her pet sayings, "I just can't be bothered about what people say and think." To me that made sense. I have more or less applied it to my mode of living, and find it helps me face a lot of would-be embarrassing situations.

After finishing Grandma's pruning, Kenneth and

An early 1930s picture of Aunt Pearl, Grandma Cook and Aunt Ida in Fresno. Pearl and Ida, Papa's sisters, were both nurses.

Walter hunted for more work in Fresno. They were told there were no jobs now, but if they hung around for another month there would be a lot of farm work available.

However, since we were on the last part of our long trip, we were all anxious to get home; and another prolonged job would delay our departing for Arizona.

Della and Kenneth were especially anxious to get to

Arizona to start housekeeping in a home of their own. After talking it over with the rest of the family, Kenneth decided to write home to his twin brother Carl, asking Carl to borrow some money and send it to Fresno. When they received the money, Kenneth and Della planned on heading for home in their own car by themselves.

There was still work to do for Uncle Bob, but Papa thought it would be better to make the trip up into the mountains first to see Grandpa Purtymun.

"When we come back to Fresno," Papa said, "I can finish Bob's garden while Walter works on my car and gets it in condition for the long drive back to Arizona."

Kenneth and Walter had been busy repairing tires and tubes and tuning up their cars. There wasn't room in one car for all of us to make the trip to see Grandpa. It would take too much money to take another car, so it was decided that the Greenwells and Bakers were to stay in Fresno and finish their mechanical work. They didn't know Grandpa Purtymun anyway.

CHAPTER TWENTY-FOUR

Brand New Shoes

Just before we left to go to North Fork, where Grandpa Purtymun lived, Grandma Cook came over and gave Aunt Ida some money and told her to take me downtown and buy a pair of girl's shoes for me to wear up to see Grandpa. I think she must have noticed how I hated to wear those old shoes that Kenneth had given me. I never wore them unless Mamma made me put them on.

I was very excited when I was told I would ride a streetcar downtown, because I had never ridden in a streetcar be-fore. I was glad too, to get the chance to see the inside of one of those big stores like the ones we had passed so often on this trip.

We had our choice of seats in the streetcar, because we caught it at the end of the line where it started back into town. We were the first people to get on.

When Aunt Ida stopped to pay our fare, she told me to go ahead of her and pick out a seat near the window. She looked a little surprised when she found I had sat down in the first seat behind the driver and that I insisted she sit by the window.

"Don't you want to sit by the window, Laura, where you can look out?" she asked.

"No," I told her, "I'd rather sit near the aisle."

"All right," she said, as she scooted over by the window.

What she didn't know was I had seen enough streets and houses in our travels. What I really wanted to see was the inside of a streetcar so I could tell the other kids about it; and I wanted to sit near the front so I could watch the people when they came up the steps.

They came in all shapes and some of them wore the funniest clothes; some were smiling and some of them looked like they would bite your head off if you touched them. In fact, I still like to sit in a public place and watch the people who walk by.

The car was bigger than I thought it would be inside. I wondered if there would ever be enough people to fill all those empty seats.

Down the full length of the car and above the window there were big signs advertising different things. I read them all, but the only one I remember had a picture of a big wood-stove on it; below the picture was the sentence, "A Kalama Zoo, Direct to You." It sort of rhymed and I kept saying it over and over. I guess that is why I still remember it. I think it was advertising a cookstove, because on the oven of the stove in the picture were the words "Kalama Zoo."

I don't recall much about the rest of the ride, except that before we climbed off, every seat was full and a lot of people were standing in the aisle holding onto straps that hung down from the roof of the car. Every time the car would stop to let people on or off, those people holding onto the straps would sway forward and backward. It must have been a rough ride, because I remember thinking that they'd all have ended up on the floor if they hadn't had the straps.

We climbed off the streetcar in the center of town. There were tall buildings, or what seemed like tall buildings to me, all around us. Some of them must have been four stories high. I was hoping we would go to the top of one of them so I could look out a window. I thought I would've been able to see all over town.

The only house with an upstairs I had been in was Grandma Cook's house in Yagar Canyon, back in Arizona. I don't remember much about that house, because I was only five years old when she lived in it. Of course I had been in the attic bedroom at Grandma Thompson's. It was where my uncles slept. It really didn't count, because it was so crowded with beds, it had no window, and it was dark. The only light it had came through a glass in the door that led to the outside stairs.

The attic bedroom where the uncles slept, seen in background. The Thompsons about 1912, back row: Uncle Green, Uncle Albert, Uncle Jimmy, Grandma (Maggie) Thompson, Uncle Charley, and Grandma's brother Jim James. Front row: Aunt Lizzie Thompson Nail and her daughters Myrtle (p. 25) and Maggie, and Grandpa Jim Thompson with Uncle Guy and Iva Nail. Uncle Frank and Uncle Fred (p. 28) have already left home.

When we walked into the first store, I didn't have time to even look around the place, because when we entered the door, instead of going upstairs we went downstairs. At the bottom of the steps we found ourselves in a big room filled with tables. The tables were covered with a variety of clothing. Aunt Ida went over to a table where there were a lot of shoes stacked. She picked up a pair of brown oxfords. Then looking at me she asked, "Do you know what size shoe you wear?"

Before I could answer, a man came over to where we were and asked me to sit down on a stool-like chair that had a footstool attached to it. He said, "Take off your shoes and I'll measure your foot."

That was the first time I ever had my foot measured like that. Back home when Mamma ordered us a new pair of shoes out of the Sears Roebuck catalog, where we got all our clothes, she put our bare foot on the back of the order blank and marked where our heel and toes were. This man had some kind of ruler-thing that had a sliding attachment that he slid up next to my toes and heel. He also had something that measured the width of my foot.

He didn't say what size shoe I wore, but he told Aunt Ida he didn't think I could wear any of the shoes on the table. He said he would see if he could find something that would fit my feet.

He brought several pairs of women's shoes back, but they were all so narrow he couldn't get my big feet into them. Finally he said to Aunt Ida, "She has such wide feet you will probably have to have special shoes made to fit her feet. If you want to, you might try the shoe store down the street. They handle nothing but shoes and they may have something in a wider size."

I guess I must have feet like my Uncle Jess, Papa's older brother. I have heard him say many times, "It takes a half a cowhide for each of my feet. The boxes my shoes come in fit my feet better than the shoes do." I

After I put on my old shoes again, we went down the street to the shoe store. It was on the ground floor, so we went neither up nor down. The room wasn't quite so big and there were shelves instead of tables. There were aisles between each row of shelves. I had never seen so many shoes. They were stacked everywhere. *Surely,* I thought, *with all those shoes, some will fit my feet.*

After measuring my feet like the other guy did, the owner of the store started bringing out shoes and trying them on my feet. None were wide enough to squeeze my feet into. Finally, in desperation, he brought out several pairs of what he called "Old Lady Comfort Shoes." The

Laura at sixteen, wearing dancing shoes. The shoes were so tight they usually wore out after one night's dancing. The dances always lasted until two or three in the morning, and sometimes 'til roosters crowed at dawn.

only pair of these horrible-looking shoes he could get my big feet into were colored a bright orange.

I guess I should have appreciated Grandma's and Aunt Ida's interest in me, but when I walked out of that store with those orange shoes on my feet, I wished I were still wearing Kenneth's shoes. They at least blended with the rest of my clothes and weren't too noticeable.

To make a bad day worse, Aunt Ida had to stop by a friend's house on the way home. This lady had canned some pickled peaches and was so proud of her canning ability that she insisted Aunt Ida and I sample the results.

The house was real fancy and she brought the peaches out on her best china. The only tool she brought to eat the peaches with was a fork. If I had been home I would've stuck the fork into the peach and chewed the flesh off down to the seed. Then I could've poked the seed in my mouth and finished it off. I sat there doing nothing, watching the two women. They started cutting their peach off the seed with the fork, and seemed to have no trouble at all. As soon as I tried it, my peach flew out of my dish, across the table, onto the hardwood floor, and came to rest in the center of a beautiful braided rug.

The lady tried to be nice and said it was all right, but as she scrubbed the waxed floor and the rug with a wet rag, I knew she wasn't thinking very nice things about me. I decided then and there, I would never try to eat a pickled peach again unless I was home.

CHAPTER TWENTY-FIVE

Grandpa Purtymun's Old Store

Grandpa <u>Purtymun</u> and Grandma Cook had separated when Aunt Ida, the youngest of their eight children, was twelve years old. I had never seen Grandpa Purtymun, because he left Arizona soon after the separation.

A few years later, Papa's mother had married Grandpa Cook, so as far back as I can remember, Grandpa Cook had been my grandpa. When Grandpa Cook passed away, I could hardly picture someone else taking his place in my life.

Months ago when Papa was planning our trip, the main reason for going to California was to see his father. Grandpa Purtymun was sixty-nine years old and Papa knew he might not have another chance to see him if we didn't visit him this time.

It was a good day's drive for us to go from Fresno to North Fork, so early one morning, Papa and all the unmarried kids and Mamma headed up the road to see Grandpa Purtymun. As we drove higher and higher into the mountains, I was secretly hoping the old Ford would

Grandpa (Steve) Purtymun, center with moustache, and Grandma (Martha) in 1891, before they separated and Grandma became Grandma Cook.

Back row: Emera P., Jess Howard (Martha's brother) and C.S. "Bear" Howard (Jess H. and Martha's dad). Front row: Jess P., Grandma, Pearl P. (in Grandma's lap), Grandpa, Charley P., Albert P. (papa) and George P. Dan P. is sitting on the floor. All the boys and Pearl are the Purtymun's children; Aunt Ida isn't born yet.

refuse to climb any higher. I felt we were wasting our time and money going in the opposite direction from our intended route back to Arizona.

It was late in the afternoon when we passed a small sawmill with a pond full of logs waiting to be put through the mill. A little later we drove by a power plant; then we started seeing lumber shacks poking out from between the pine trees on the steep hillside. I guessed we must have been in North Fork, when Papa pulled the car off the road and ground to a stop in front of one of these shacks.

"This must be the place," he said. "It looks like it's been a store." No one had told me Grandpa owned a store. Of course this building didn't look much like a store when you compared it with the many stores we had seen since we left home. I learned later Grandpa didn't run a store anymore, but he was living in the same building he had used as a store.

This building was a little different from the other shacks we had passed. It had a porch completely across the front of it, and the porch was covered with a shed roof. Above the porch roof, on a false front, was printed the word "STORE." It was almost impossible to make out the letters because most of the paint had peeled off the weather-beaten boards.

At one end of the porch were some homemade wood chairs. I could almost picture some old men sitting there squirting tobacco juice on the porch-boards as they aimed at the ground several feet below.

The country around here was so steep, all the buildings were built on sloping hillsides. They had stilts holding up one end of them, while the other end rested on the ground.

The steps leading up to the porch and front door were wide and well-worn. As we started climbing out of the pickup, a little old man with a big nose opened the door and came out onto the porch. He was soon followed by a lady in a floor-length dress. Her grey hair was braided and rolled around the top of her head like a cinnamon roll.

I had seen pictures of Grandpa Purtymun, but as I stood there looking up at him, I couldn't imagine that little old man being my Grandpa. All the Purtymuns I knew were tall. If this is Grandpa, I thought, all their children must have inherited Grandma's height.

Suddenly the little man exclaimed, "Albert!" and he started shuffling down the steps. Papa's face lit up with a big grin and he pushed ahead of the rest of us.

When they met halfway up the stairs, they clamped their hands together and just stood there looking at each other. I think they forgot all about the rest of us, they were so wrapped up in their feelings.

When I saw the way Papa greeted his Dad, I started feeling guilty for my thoughts about coming up here to see Grandpa.

At last Papa let go of Grandpa's hand and let Mamma and the rest of us say hello. Then we all went up the steps and greeted Grandpa's wife.

I guess this lady had a name, but since this was the only time we ever saw her, I don't remember what it was. After this visit when any of us mentioned her, we always referred to her as Grandpa's wife.

We had hardly entered the building when Mamma sent Papa back to the car to get the pot of beans she had cooked and brought along with us. She said, "We'll get supper out of the way and then we can visit."

I figured the big room we had entered had originally been the store. The only windows were the two on either side of the door. They were covered with curtains now, but earlier I'll bet there had been signs advertising Arbuckle Coffee, Bull Durham Tobacco, and Clabber Girl Baking Powder.

Through a door in the back of this room, I could see a big wood cookstove. Before I could think of an excuse to go into the room and look around, Papa came back with the beans, and Mamma and Grandpa's wife went

Grandpa Purtymun's Old Store

through the door to prepare our evening meal. I knew then I had better stay out of the way or I would get bawled out.

In a short time Mamma came to the door and said, "Get washed up if you want anything to eat."

It hadn't taken them long to fix that meal. All they had to do was make some biscuits and set the table, while the beans were warming. After we ate, Grandpa went into a small pantry-like storeroom and brought out some hard candy for dessert. I guessed that it was candy they had left over after they quit running the store. They had probably saved it for special occasions, like our coming to see them.

At first I had been disappointed in the way Grandpa Purtymun looked, but by the end of the evening I decided he wasn't so bad. Maybe he wasn't tall, but he sure had the Purtymun personality. He treated us kids like we were people instead of nuisances that had to be tolerated. He talked to us and made jokes and didn't bawl us out.

As soon as supper was over and the dishes washed, Grandpa's wife went upstairs to their bedroom. She said she would leave Grandpa's family for him to enjoy. I felt she was using that as an excuse to get away from us noisy kids, but later I learned that this was customary in their home. When her people came to visit, Grandpa went off and left them to visit.

In the living room there was an old sofa that made into a bed. Papa brought our bedding up from the car and Mamma made their bed on it. We kids took quilts and slept on the floor.

Papa, Mamma, and Grandpa went into the kitchen after we kids were bedded down. I have no idea how long they sat up talking, because the first thing I knew it was morning and Mamma was waking up all four of us kids. She told us to hurry, as breakfast was ready and Papa wanted to start back to Fresno as soon as we could.

CHAPTER TWENTY-SIX

Oil Strips 'Cross the Desert

Soon after our return to Fresno, Kenneth received the money for which he had written his brother Carl. Carl had borrowed the money from Pete Valazza, an old friend who owned a small grocery store in Smelter City.

I had never realized how important Arizona was to me until Della and Kenneth started talking about going home and Virgie decided to go with them. I became so homesick I asked Mamma if I could go with Della and Kenneth too. Of course the answer was, "No. You'll have to wait until Dad and I can go."

After the Greenwells and Virgie left, Papa finished the work for Uncle Bob. Walter was busy getting our car in shape for the long trip home. We were all hoping our cars would hold together until we could get across the many miles of desert we had to drive through before we were once more in our home state of Arizona.

I don't remember much of importance happening along the road after we left Fresno. We did pass through a farming settlement called Bakersfield. I wondered about this town's strange name, because Walter's last name was Baker, so I asked Walter if his family had owned the place.

"No. My people all came from the other direction. I was born in Austin, Texas," he told me. Leaving Bakersfield we drove over the Tehachapi Mountains. For experi-

Della, reading the newspaper, and Virgie, eating.on an outing around 1931; Charley gives a wise look.

enced travelers like we were, these mountains gave us no trouble at all. We had to spend only one night in them.

On the other side of the mountain we came into the desert. It was a good thing it was still cool weather, or we might have had some trouble with our tires. Our cars, too, were not too dependable, and we had some two hundred miles to go before we reached the Colorado River and would start gaining altitude.

It was warm enough m the desert, though, that Papa could roll up the canvas sides on our tent-like car-top. He thought by having an opening on each side of the truck, maybe we kids wouldn't fight so much over the limited space behind the seat. The windshield was the only opening we could look through in our home-made top. With Mamma and Papa in the seat and Chuckles sitting between them, it had been no easy task for us to see anything outside our dungeon-like confinement.

There was very little to see or enjoy as we bounced along this dry, treeless country; but it did help some to just look out at the sky or ground.

We spent one night in Barstow. It was just a small railroad town at that time. For us, Barstow was only a spot where we could buy some more gas and stock up on our dwindling supply of water.

Somewhere between Barstow and Needles, California we drove through some sand flats where the sand was so deep that in places several hundred feet across, narrow strips of oil had been laid down for the wheels of the cars to roll on. These strips were only about one foot wide, and if the driver didn't keep his car wheels on the oil his car was apt to get stuck. Our drivers were good drivers, so we made it across all right.

Several years ago I was talking to a man who came across this desert country in nineteen hundred and twenty. He said at that time every car that drove across these flats carried a roll of chicken-mesh wire. They rolled this wire across the sand and drove on it so their tires wouldn't sink into the sand.

These oil strips we crossed were probably the forerunner of all the paved roads we have today. The main traveled roads in the twenties and thirties were only topped with some kind of dirt mixture that didn't get slick when it rained, and be-came hard enough when dry to prevent the car wheels from sinking into the ground and becoming stuck. This type of road was called a surfaced road.

Laura, about seventeen years old, traveling a surfaced road on the way to Payson, Arizona. Vehicle is her first Model-T, a pickup bought from Papa.

When we made this trip I doubt if any of the roads were surfaced except near towns. Things have really changed in the last fifty years. I can hardly picture the tourist of today driving down the narrow, rough, dusty roads we traveled on; or even driving one of our old cars.

At that time the top speed of most cars was twenty-five miles an hour. The vehicles we drove seldom went that fast unless they were going down a hill. The roads were so rough that if you drove faster than fifteen miles an hour, all the bolts would shake out of the car and maybe a few vertebrae in your back would jar loose.

In my reminiscing through the past, I doubt if we met more than a dozen cars on the whole trip across the desert. Today on the freeway, I would hate to have to count the cars that come through in just an hour.

CHAPTER TWENTY-SEVEN

The Sky is Falling

We were just outside Needles when Papa pulled off the road into a likely-looking camping spot. "Does this suit you for a night's camp, Mom?" Papa asked as he braked to a stop.

"It looks as good as any I've seen since we started across this desert," Mamma answered, as she climbed out of the car and lifted Chuckles down beside her. "You kids go down into that dry wash and see what you can find for wood."

Violet, Bud and I took off running toward the dry wash Mamma had indicated with a look and turn of her head.

I heard Papa suggest something to Walter as they started unloading the stuff we would need for the night. "Don't you think we'd better pitch the tents tonight, Walt? I don't like the looks of that sky."

They both stopped working and looked up at the dark clouds that were rapidly filling the sky. "Yeah," Walter replied. "We'd better prepare for the worst. I've heard it seldom rains in Needles, but when it does you'd better look out. "

For just an overnight camp we never bothered to pitch the tents unless it was raining or looked like it might rain.

Mamma had the fire going with the sticks of wood and scraps of boards we kids had brought. The fire was cracking and snapping as if the wood was made of firecrackers.

I could hear Mamma talking above the noise of the fire. It seemed the nearer we got to home the more her thoughts traveled ahead of her body as she anxiously planned where we would live and what we would do when this trip was over. Now, as she rattled on, I didn't know if she was talking to Erma or just thinking out loud.

"In that letter I got from Mamma, Fred was still boss of the county road crew on the Oak Creek road. The camp is at Bootlegger Flat. That's not far from the old Purtymun place. They're moving the road to the other side of the creek and cutting out two crossings — it's a good thing. Erma, stir those potatoes. I'll get Dad to see Charley Allen in the morning. He owns the Purtymun place now. If it's not rented, he'd probably rent it to us. With all the fruit, and Dad working for the county, we ought to get straightened out before winter. In a little place like Needles, we should have no trouble finding his picture-taking place."

Charley Allen, a surveyor, had come west from Ohio in eighteen eighty-two. He first saw Oak Creek Canyon while working for a railroad survey crew. Later, because of illness, he had to give up his engineering career, and so he moved to Needles and became a photographer. Every summer when it was too hot for comfort in his studio in Needles, he would come back and spend a few months in the Canyon.

The Sky is Falling

The second bridge at Slide Rock in Oak Creek Canyon, then called the Falls Bridge. It washed out in the flood of March 3, 1938

When he found the old Purtymun place had never been proved up on, he immediately went through the necessary procedures to acquire the ranch. He received the deed to the property in nineteen hundred thirteen.

While camping in the Canyon he became acquainted and was a close friend of both the Thompson and the Purtymun families.

I think both of our families owe Charley Allen a big thank you for what few photographs we have of our past generations.

Once more, Mamma stopped her stream of conversational plans and turned to the present problem of getting the meal served. "You kids quit running through and kicking up dust!" she yelled at us. Then turning to Erma, who was busy getting our plates and tools out of a box, she said, "Are those potatoes done, Erma? If they are, we'd better eat, so we can get to bed before it gets dark or that storm strikes."

We kids quit playing tag and headed for the washpan. It never took long after Mamma said the word for everybody to grab their plates and begin eating.

After the dishes were washed and the beds made inside the tent, everything that water could damage or the wind blow away was put back into the car or stowed away in our tents.

Before she crawled into bed, Mamma looked around for a final checkup to see if we had missed anything; then with a "Thank God we were spared a good drenching before we got bedded down," she retired for the night.

When I came into the tent to go to bed, Violet and Bud were having their nightly argument about whose turn it was to sleep at the foot of the bed. Virgie was the cause of all this commotion, because when she had been with us both little kids had to sleep "with the feet," as we always called sleeping at the foot of the bed. When you slept "with the feet," you always had the feet of the big people sticking in your face, no matter which way you turned. Bud finally crawled into the bottom of the bed; but it was some time before I could go to sleep because of Violet's constant wiggling.

We were all sound asleep, when some time late in the night the wind came up and blew all the clouds away. A strong gust of wind hit our tent so hard it caused the center pole to poke through the top of the tent. Our tent was sixteen feet square and fourteen feet high. That was a lot of canvas to collapse on our sleeping bodies.

Unless you have had a similar experience, it would be hard for you to understand the sensation I had when I was rudely awakened by that canvas hitting me in the face. I felt like Chicken Little must have felt when the acorn hit him on the head. I was sure the sky had fallen. Chicken Little was one of the stories all of us kids heard over and over when we went to school in the one-room schoolhouse, where all eight grades were taught by one teacher. I think the story was in the third grade reader; but we heard it each year as different children entered the third grade.

I remember yelling, "Mamma!" as I clawed my way out of bed and from one fold of canvas into another fold. I felt like I was smothering. No air, no light, nothing familiar to hold onto. I could hear the kids crying on all sides of me. I must have climbed over Violet, because I heard the muffled sound of her squalling as I frantically went over something big. I was sure it was the end of the Purtymun Clan.

I heard Papa say later, "I thought I would never find my way out of bed and get out from under that canvas so I could pull that tent off those squalling kids."

Papa will never know what a relief it was to me either, when he got that tent off my head and I could see the sky was still up there with the stars still twinkling.

We were all scared but no one was hurt; so after we calmed down we went back to sleep with only the sky for our roof.

In the morning we were anxious to be moving on toward home, so we stopped in Needles just long enough to buy supplies and see Mr. Allen. He was happy to see us and told us he would be glad to let us move onto his place. He told us the orchard and everything was in a run-down condition, but if we would put the water in the ditch after the spring floods and prune the orchard, that would be more than enough work to pay for the rent.

We left Needles in high spirits, happy at the thought of reaching home soon. When we reached the Colorado River south of Needles and I could see the river, thick with mud and rushing under the bridge in its spring flooding stage, it looked terrible to me. I was glad we had a bridge to cross instead of an old ferry. I asked Mamma if this was the place where Grandpa Thompson operated the ferry.

"No," she answered. "That was miles above here."

When Grandpa Thompson, Mamma's father, first came to Arizona in about eighteen seventy, he owned and operated a ferry across the Colorado River. His ferry was somewhere below where the Virgin River emptied into the Colorado River. He later sold the ferry to a man by the name of Bonella, and then Grandpa came to central Arizona to settle.

This was the first time Mamma or any of us kids had ever been in the western part of our state. I was surprised to find the country looked almost the same after we crossed the bridge into Arizona as it looked in California. There was very little vegetation, and the ground was just as level and desolate-looking. We did climb into some mountains and go through two prosperous-looking mining towns, Oatman and Goldfield, not too long after we entered Arizona.

I guess our old cars were as anxious to get home as we were, because they ran trouble-free from early morning until dark everyday, carrying us closer to home with each passing mile.

CHAPTER TWENTY-EIGHT

No Brakes on Mingus Mountain

When we reached Yagar Canyon, on the west side of Mingus Mountain, we camped on a small flat beside the road. Just below our camp and in the bottom of the canyon on a large flat, we could see Grandma Cook's old home. We hurried through our evening meal and bed-making so Mamma and we kids could go down and look over the place.

After all these years, the house and windmill are still being used by the Fain Land and Cattle Company. I don't know when the house was built, but my Grandma and Grandpa Cook owned the place and operated the cattle ranch when I was born in nineteen ten. It is now nineteen seventy-nine and when I stopped by the house yesterday to take some pictures, I found a family living there who worked for the Fain's. The windmill can easily be seen from the highway as you drive from Jerome to Prescott on Highway 89-A. It is on the left side of the road and at the mouth of Yagar Canyon, where the canyon leaves the mountains and opens up into Lonesome Valley.

Grandma Cook's old home at the bottom of Yagar (Yaeger) Canyon as it looked in fall, 1979.

As we now approached the place, we could see the windmill with its rustic blades turning and the water trough near the tower running over. Although the ranch house looked much the same as I remembered it, the curtainless windows indicated that there was no one living there. The border of quart beer bottles Grandma had buried neck down in the dirt with two inches of the bottle bottom showing above ground to hold the gravel she had placed on the walk, were still edging the path that led to the front door. Most of the fruit trees were dead from neglect or old age. We could see parts of the stumps and dead limbs of the many rose bushes Grandma had planted with loving care around the house.

As we were leaving, Mamma told us the people who owned the place now had probably moved into town and used the house for a place to stay only when they were checking on their cattle.

On the way back to camp Mamma told us about a Christmas not long after she and Papa were married, when all the members of the family gathered at Grandma's house here in Yagar Canyon to celebrate the holiday. Great Uncle Jess Howard, Grandma's only brother and a bachelor, had consumed too many quarts

Grandma Cook in the early 1930s after she had returned from Fresno to settle in Oak Creek Canyon. She lived with her oldest son Emera in a house by the creek, across from what is now the Red Rock Lodge.

of beer, and while playing the accordion he became so excited he pulled the instrument apart in the middle. Everybody laughed when they saw the look on his face as he looked down and found he was holding half the accordion in each hand.

I didn't know Uncle Jess Howard very well, because after I was born at Red Rock, south of Sedona, my parents moved over near Dewey. Papa started homesteading a place on Yar-brough Wash, where we lived until I was eight years old. During that period of my life we came back to Oak Creek and Sedona on an occasional visit. When we moved back to Sedona in nineteen eight-

Grandma Cook's son, Uncle Jess Purtymun, carries on the accordion tradition. He was named after Grandma's brother, Great Uncle Jess Howard (see family portrait, p. 140), who once pulled his instrument apart. Grandma Cook stands with hand on hip; other son Emera holds gun. Photo taken around 1941.

een, Uncle Jess came to our home for Christmas. He brought each of us kids a store-bought present. That was the first time I remember seeing Uncle Jess, and that was the first present I received that wasn't homemade. I always thought of Uncle Jess as a nice, quiet fellow. I just couldn't picture him ever getting drunk. In nineteen and eight he had homesteaded the property where Garland's Resort now stands in Oak Creek Canyon. He never married, and lived so far from any neighbor, I guess he thought it was all right to go on a little spree once in awhile.

When we reached our camp after our little excursion, Papa and Walter were discussing the condition of our car, especially the brakes.

I heard Papa say to Walter, "Walt, I think you had better tighten the bands on my car before we start over Mingus in the morning. I'd sure hate to start over that mountain with no more brakes than I had when we stopped here."

"I'll tighten them before we leave. After traveling over most of the Western United States, it would be kind of silly taking the chance of having a serious accident when we are practically home."

On a Model-T there were three pedals on the floorboard. The first one was called the clutch. If you pressed it all the way down, you were in low gear. The second pedal was the reverse gear. When you wanted to go backward, you had to press the clutch pedal halfway down to put the car in neutral, and also push the second or reverse pedal down before your car was in reverse. The third pedal was the brake. When you were driving a lot in mountainous country, all three pedals were used as a brake. If one pedal was pressed for too long a time, it became hot and soon burned the rubber-like covering off the band, and you would find yourself without any means of stopping your vehicle.

The covering on our bands was probably worn quite thin, but the menfolks thought that by tightening them we could get home all right.

Mingus Mountain, the mountain Papa. was concerned about driving over without brakes, is a small range of mountains in central Arizona. In order to reach the Verde Valley where Smelter City (our destination) was located, we had no choice but to go over the mountain. Anyone who is afraid of mountain roads should never drive over Mingus Mountain. The road follows Yagar Canyon to a high pass over seven thousand feet. In some places the road is very crooked, steep and narrow as it winds its way across the many side canyons along its path. Driving down on the east side of the mountain, the road is about twice as far and much scarier than it was coming up to the pass. It follows first one canyon then another until it finally winds up on the rim of the Jerome Gulch. About one mile before entering Jerome, the road is perched upon a narrow ledge several feet above the sheer drop to the bottom of the Gulch. Since Jerome is built on the steep slope of the mountain, each street through the town is several terraces above the next street below. Some of the streets are paved in washboard ripples of concrete, in order to give a car more traction to climb the steep grade.

Leaving Jerome the road continues down the mountain-side until it reaches Clarkdale, Cottonwood, and Smelter City on the bank of the Verde River.

When we bedded down for our last night out, everyone seemed restless. I could hear them tossing and turning. I imagined they were worrying about going over Mingus without brakes. I wasn't the least bit concerned, because I was sure our menfolks could take care of any difficulty. They had proven this many times since we had left home. I lay awake a long time, but I was visualizing what it would be like to be home again. I wondered if the trees, the mountains, the Verde River, and Oak Creek would look the same as they had when we had left them eight months ago. When I heard a coyote howl somewhere in the distance I wasn't afraid, because I told myself it was only an Arizona coyote that was sending its greeting out to welcome us home.

I awakened to the sound of breaking wood and the snapping and popping of the campfire. At first I couldn't remember where I was as I looked around in the shadowy dawn. I could see Papa's outline as he walked back and forth between the stack of wood and the blazing fire. All at once it came to me: we were in Yagar Canyon and would reach home today. I can't remember any time when I was more excited about something happening. I immediately rose and began digging under my pillow for my clothes. By the time I was dressed, a rosy glow was showing over Mingus Mountain where the sun would later make its appearance.

As if some magic had been added to this special day, everybody began scrambling for his clothes in the semi-darkness. Violet couldn't find her overalls and accused me of losing them. The mystery was solved when Bud exclaimed, "Oh, heck! These pants aren't mine. They're away too big." He was standing up fastening the suspenders to the buttons on the bib of the overalls, when he discovered the suspenders were much too long and the seat of the pants reached down to his knees.

"Guess I got your old pants, Violet, but where's mine?" he mumbled.

"Open up your eyes. Can't you see them laying over there in plain sight? Hurry up and get out of my pants. I'm freezing," Violet grumbled.

As soon as everyone had gotten out of bed, Mamma turned to Violet and me and said, "You kids can fold the bedding up while I cook breakfast, and I don't want to hear any more squabbling. Do you hear!"

"Yes, Mamma," I answered as I grabbed a quilt and yelled, "Violet; get hold of the other end of this and help."

She did as I said, but growled back at me, "You're not my boss."

As soon as breakfast was over and the dishes washed, Mamma started packing our things and putting them into the truck. When everything was in its place, she turned to Erma and said, "If you'll keep Chuckles,

Laura and I will take Violet and Bud and start walking on up the road. I hate to stand around and wait for our men. They're just alike.

They're standing over there now rolling smokes. They act as if they've got all day to fix our car, and they probably won't do anything until they finish smoking."

Erma said, "Sure, I'll keep Chuckles." Chuckles, hearing his name spoken, jumped up from where he and Bud had been busy building a corral for some pop-ball cows they had gathered from a nearby oak bush.

Violet, about fifteen, acting silly with her cousin Lee, left (Fred Thompson's son — see p.28), who is wearing her coat, and Guy, Mamma's youngest brother (p. 135). Site is just below present-day Encinoso picnic Area in Oak Creek Canyon, where the road used to go through this man-made tunnel. When the road was oiled and widened, the tunnel was removed.

Pop-balls were one of the Purtymun children's favorite toys. They are a round pink and sometimes striped growth that can be found on the leaves of oak bush. When first picked they are soft, and when squashed they make a popping noise. I guess that is where they got the name of pop-balls. We used to thread them on strings to make necklaces. Also we poked tiny sticks into them to make arms and legs. Then by putting a small ball on the end of a stick and inserting it into the body ball, we had the neck and head of our pop-ball men. We used them for all types of farm animals, depending on their size and what we were playing. Now the kids were using them for cows.

Bud gathered his share of "cattle" and poked them into his pocket. Then he joined the rest of us hikers as we started up the road.

We were probably halfway up the mountain when a guy driving a big truck stopped and asked us if we wanted to ride. Boy, was I glad, because I had been carrying Bud piggyback for the last mile. He had become tired and asked Mamma if we could wait until Papa came along, but she said no, that I could carry him. We all got into the truck and continued the climb up the mountain.

When we reached the pass where the road started down on the Jerome side of the mountain, our driver pulled to the side of the road and stopped.

"I would like to let you ride on into Jerome, but the company I work for won't let me carry passengers down this hill," he said.

"Oh, that's all right," Mamma said as we kids scrambled out of the truck and she stepped carefully to the ground. "Our men ought to be along soon. I sure thank you for bringing us to the top of the hill. It was a big help."

The original pass at this spot over Mingus Mountain was only a trail. After a steep plunge down the mountain it followed a canyon, crossing the dry-wash bed from time to time. In this way it took advantage of the narrow flats on either side of the canyon.

Years ago on one of the larger flats there had been a small settlement called Mescal. It amounted to nothing more than several tent-houses, some dugouts in the bank of the hillside and a few lumber shacks scattered along the trail.

In eighteen ninety Grandpa Thompson, Mamma's father, had taken a contract to do some freighting for the mine in Jerome. He didn't want to leave his family alone on their isolated farm at Indian Gardens in Oak Creek Canyon, so he leased the farm out and moved his wife and children to the ranch of a friend named Haskal. The Haskal ranch is located west of where the Yavapai College now stands, and it was only a short distance from where the original trail came down the mountain.

The Thompson family lived here on the Verde Valley side of Mingus Mountain until it began to get hot as summer advanced. Then Grandpa moved them up to Mescal where it was cooler. Mamma was only three years old that summer, but she thought she could locate the place where they had camped if she could find something that looked familiar.

A few years later in eighteen ninety-eight Grandpa Cook, Papa's stepfather, was operating a small sawmill in Mescal when his first wife Sadie passed away. She was the only person, so I've been told, who was buried in Mescal.

Much later in nineteen four, after Mamma and Papa were married, Papa worked for Grandpa Cook cutting timber for the stulls Grandpa made in his mill. Stulls are timbers used in mines to prevent cave-ins. Papa and Mamma lived up in the pass at that time, and had made many trips up and down the trail. Mamma told us that on one of these trips they had spent the night in Mescal and had made their bed in the sawdust pile by the mill. She was sure she could still find the place her parents

Grandma and Grandpa Thompson in Indian Gardens around 1905.

Grandma Thompson in about 1933, still living at the Thompson homestead in Indian Gardens, where Grandpa had first built a log cabin in 1876.

had pitched their tent so many years ago; and maybe if she was lucky she could find the grave of Grandpa's wife.

Anything that sounded like adventure was what we kids liked, so we left the road where we had been walking and were soon at the bottom of the canyon following the old trail. We came to the spot where we found what was left of the old sawdust pile where the mill had been. Later we discovered a few rocks in rows and we decided that they were what was left of the foundations of the lumber buildings. Here and there we spotted an old washtub or coal-oil can, crumpled up and showing the result of years out in the weather. At last we came to the spot Mamma felt sure was where their tent had been pitched. Now we were ready to look for the grave. Right in the middle of our exploring, Mamma called us kids to where she stood and in a half-whisper said, "There's a man with a burro coming down the trail toward us. Hurry! Let's get away from here and up closer to the road before he gets any closer."

I was disappointed that we had to leave when things were beginning to look interesting, but from the sound of Mamma's voice I figured we'd better get away from there. I don't know why we were afraid, but I guess our looking for a grave and being many miles from anything that looked civilized made us all a little spooky.

We hurried across the flat and began climbing the steep hill back up to the road. When I paused to get my breath and had time to look back, I could see the man and his burro slowly going on down the trail.

We reached the top and continued our journey by following the road the rest of the way. We were almost into Jerome before Walter and Papa caught up with us. Papa was driving Walter's car and was in the lead. We had walked down the last steep hill before entering Jerome, so Walter stopped the car he was driving and let us ride.

As we scrambled into the car he told us, "The bands

on Dad's car were so thin, I wouldn't let him drive it. I figured, me being younger, maybe I could jump a little quicker if it became necessary. I think now it'll be safe for you to ride from here until we reach those steep streets in Jerome." We all quickly climbed aboard.

I didn't mind at all when Walter let us out in Jerome. Walking down the familiar streets, I could look down on the pleasant valley through which the tree-lined Verde River winds. I could see the two stacks of the Clarkdale smelter, with the smoke boiling up into the clear sky. To

Laura, sixteen, at home in Oak Creek Canyon on the site of present-day Manzanita Campground. The Purtymuns lived at this location for thirteen years, longer than they lived anywhere else.

the south the lone stack of the Clemenceau smelter appeared to be the same as it did when we had left it many months ago. Far to the north the snow-capped San Francisco Peaks looked like a giant ice cream cone poking up into the sky above the darker, pine-covered high country. Nearer, but still miles away, I could see the Red Rock Country near Sedona. The sight of all this brought to me such pleasant memories I could hardly hold myself back. I wanted to run the rest of the way home. This was the first time in my life that I felt that strange homecoming feeling I get when, after a long absence, I return home. I felt like I wanted to gather the whole country into my arms and hold it forever.

When we reached the foot of the Jerome Hill, Walter and Papa were waiting for us. As we all climbed aboard the old jalopy, Walter said, "I've never taken such a nerve-wracking ride in my life. Dad stayed as near as he dared in front of me, hoping if my brakes went out completely, he could hold back both cars by setting his own brakes."

CHAPTER TWENTY-NINE

Tea and Sandwiches

We were soon through Clarkdale and into Cottonwood where Papa and Walter parked in front of the only garage in town. Mamma sat in the car for only a minute after the men disappeared into the garage. She pushed herself out of the car seat, and stepping to the ground, she walked over to where Erma and Chuckles sat in Walter's car.

"I think I'll take the kids and walk on to Smelter City," she said. "It's only a couple of miles to the Halberg house where Della and Kenneth are. On the way I'll stop at Siler's store and pick up a loaf of bread and something for lunch. I didn't have my tea at noon and now my head is killing me. It must be after three o'clock. I don't know why I always develop a headache if I don't get my tea. It don't seem to bother our men if they completely miss their lunches. Chuckles will be all right with you, Erma?"

"Oh, yes, Chuckles is all right, aren't you, punk?" Erma said. Chuckles snuggled up close to Erma as we started walking on down the street.

Tea and Sandwiches

I was just as anxious as Mamma to move on, and from the way Violet and Bud started running down the street I think they were ready to hurry on, too.

It didn't take Mamma long to get what she wanted from the store, and so we were soon on our way out of Cottonwood. As we hurried along on foot, we were all hoping we would find Della or someone at home when we reached our destination.

Creola was hanging clothes in the backyard when she saw us walking up the road. Creola and Della were sisters-in-law, having married brothers, Kenneth and Carl. She rushed into the house where Della was and yelled excitedly, "Della, I see your Mother and the kids coming up the road walking. I didn't see a sign of the rest of the family. I wonder why they're walking?"

Della dropped the shirt she was mending and rushed to the door just as we entered the yard. Opening the door she asked, "Where did you guys come from? Where's Papa and the cars? Did something happen?"

"Nothing has happened, Della," Mamma said. "There's something wrong with the brakes of our car so the men stopped at the garage to get whatever they needed to fix them. Do you have any hot water? We haven't had anything to eat since breakfast. The kids and me walked most of the way from Yagar Canyon and me with no tea at noon, my head started aching. That's why we walked from the garage up here so I could get a cup of hot tea and the kids could have a sandwich."

"You haven't had lunch yet?" Creola asked as she held the door open for us to enter. "I'll bet you'd like a peanut butter or jelly sandwich," she said, as she smiled at Violet and Bud.

We entered the living room, but soon moved on into the kitchen where the teakettle was boiling away on the big wood-range.

"All I need is a cup of hot tea to ease this headache," Mamma said. "I have some lunch stuff here I

172　　　　　　　　　　　　　　　　　　　TRAVELING BY TIN LIZZIE

Main Street, Cottonwood, six years before the Purtymuns pulled into town at the end of their nine-month western tour. The only garage in town is seen at right, just beyond the pool hall; gas pump stands out front, near smaller shed.

Tea and Sandwiches

bought at the store in Cottonwood." Placing the sack on the table, Mamma accepted the cup of tea Creola gave her, and as she sat down she added, "Don't go to any trouble, Creola, all we need are sandwiches."

I felt like I could eat about six sandwiches myself. I looked around and not seeing Kenneth, I figured he must be working. Well, I wouldn't have to fight him for whatever was put out to eat, I thought.

As Mamma sipped her tea and Della and Creola made sandwiches, Della brought us up to date on the happenings around here.

"Kenneth went to work the day after he applied for a job in the smelter. He's working the afternoon shift and won't be home until midnight; Virgie rode out to Indian Gardens with the mailman last week. She plans on staying with Grandma until you come home." (The post office was in Grandma Thompson's home).

The coffee was ready to drink and the sandwiches all made when we heard the cars drive up with the rest of the gang. They were soon washed up and ready to join us with our belated lunch.

I think we all felt better with our stomachs full once more. The men went right out and started working on our car.

While the ladies were cleaning up our lunch mess, Mamma told Della about us stopping to see Mr. Allen in Needles to ask if we could move onto his place for the summer. I could see Mamma was making some plans about our future.

"Dad doesn't want to work in the smelter anymore and we're all tired of city life. He and Walter both think they can go to work for the county on one of the road jobs; but of course there's a lot of work to be done on the old Purtymun place before Dad can go to work anywhere."

"I hate to tell you this, Mamma," Della interrupted Mamma's talk. "But after those people who were living in our house moved out, someone broke into the bedroom where we had all our stuff stored. I went up there to check on the place and found the door open. The only thing I could find missing was your big trunk. Remember the one where you stored all your keepsakes?"

"Not my big trunk!" Mamma exclaimed. "I've had that trunk ever since Dad and I were first married. So many of my pictures and everything were in it."

I thought for a minute Mamma was going to cry, but she gained control of herself. "It's hard for me to believe someone would do a thing like that."

"But it's true, and it was your trunk, Mamma," Della said. "I inquired around the neighborhood and found out whoever took the trunk dumped it and tried to burn the stuff; and then they sold the trunk. My informant told me the culprit was a man, and that he did the burning down by that old tunnel below our house. I went down to where it had been burned, and sure enough, I recognized some of the stuff that wouldn't burn. It was the things out of your trunk all right, Mamma."

"He sure must have been hard-up for money to do a thing like that," Erma said.

That old trunk had been part of our family for many years. It was almost like losing a member of our household, like an old dog or something we had all learned to love. I felt like Mamma. I could hardly believe it was true. I remembered how we kids would be so happy when Mamma opened the trunk to get something out and we would yell to each other, "Come quick! Mamma is opening the big trunk."

Later the woman who bought the trunk heard the story of how it had been stolen. She sent word to Mamma that if Mamma would give her back the three dollars she'd paid for the trunk, Mamma could have it.

We got the trunk back all right, but I guess Mamma was past the keepsake-saving age, because after that she used the trunk as a storage place for flour and sugar to keep the mice from eating them.

It was dark before the menfolk could complete the job of putting the new brake bands on our car, so we had to spend the night at Carl and Creola's place. As Kenneth wouldn't be home until midnight, Della came out and joined our campfire group. She told us that as soon as she and Kenneth could save enough money to buy a cookstove and a few other articles they would need for housekeeping, they were going to move to a place of their own. She said, "I'm so tired of sleeping, and you might say living, in the back of that strip-down; I'd feel like a queen just to be able to stretch out in a real bed once more. . . and it really'd be nice to find something without having to dig through a dozen boxes."

After a minute's thought Mamma said, "I'm sure that house we're going to move into on Oak Creek will have everything we'll need. Why don't you and Kenneth take what you can use out of our house here in Smelter City? There's no need of leaving anything else there to be either stolen or burned."

"I think we might sell the place anyway, since we won't be living there anymore." Papa added his opinion to Mamma's. "You might just as well use it until you can buy stuff of your own."

"Sounds like a good idea," Della said. "I'll talk it over with Kenneth."

I didn't get to hear the result of that conversation, because Mamma made me go to bed before Kenneth came home. I didn't mind much though, because I went to sleep thinking of the fun I would have swimming and everything in Oak Creek this summer.

CHAPTER THIRTY

What Happened After

Della and Kenneth, with our furniture, soon moved up into one of the company houses. Much later, in nineteen thirty-three, they bought part of Kenneth's parents' ranch and moved out on lower Oak Creek at Cornville. Kenneth is now retired and they are still living in the same house they moved into forty-seven years ago, although the house has been remodeled several times through the years. They were blessed with three daughters, Virginia, Patsy and Kay, who are all living nearby.

We spent the first summer after our return from the trip on the old Purtymun Place. Violet, Bud and I went to summer school at the Upper Oak Creek schoolhouse. For many years we had to have summer school in the Canyon, because during the winter months when it flooded, the children who lived on the opposite side of the creek couldn't get to school for days at a time because there were no bridges. After school was out that fall, we moved up to the head of the Canyon where Papa was boss of the county road crew that built the only bridge that crossed Oak Creek in that part of the Canyon. Papa bought a small tent to be used for a kitchen, and we used our circus tent for a living room-bedroom combination. While we were living here Zola, the last member of the Purtymun family, was born on November eighteenth, nineteen twenty-five.

What Heppened After

Although Mamma and Papa moved many times during their remaining years together, they never again mentioned leaving Arizona to look for a better place to live.

After Papa retired in the middle of the nineteen forties, Mamma and Papa bought part of the Thompson estate.

In the beginning the Thompson estate consisted of three hundred and twenty acres of land. Mr. and Mrs. Jim Thompson, my Mother's parents, each used their

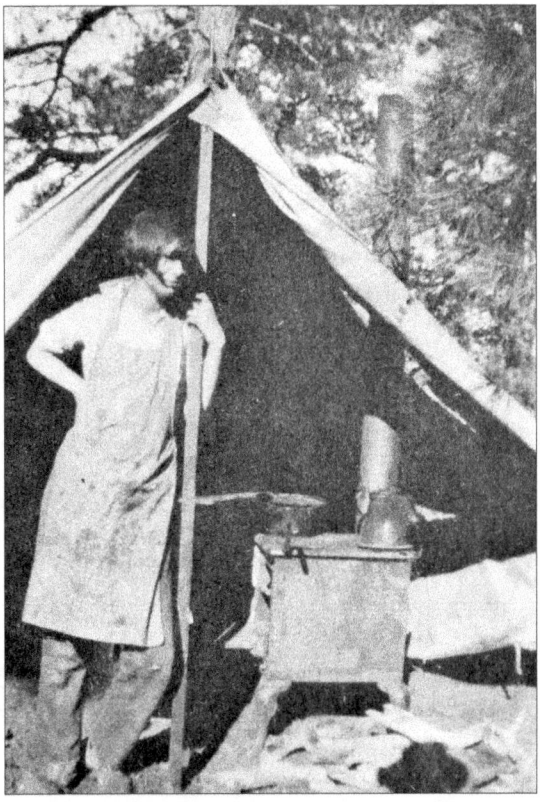

1928: Laura at Munds Park, Arizona, standing in the tent-kitchen the Purtymuns had used since Papa bought it the autumn after the trip.

Zola, the youngest Purtymun, around 1929.

homestead rights to acquire the property extending from where the Twin Oaks Tavern, the Oak Creek Terrace Motel, and the Creekside Mobil Village are, down both sides of the creek to about one-half mile below the Indian Gardens Store. The home of the Thompson family and most of the farming ground they used was across the creek from where the state placed the historical marker.

The ground Mamma and Papa bought was where Grandpa Thompson had built his first log cabin before he was married. It is located a half-mile north of the Indian Gardens' Store, but is on the opposite side of the creek. Here is where Mamma and Papa built a rock house, planted fruit trees, blackberries, and a garden. They spent their summer months farming, but as soon as they had their crops harvested and it became cool in the desert, they would leave the Canyon and go south to spend the winter where it was warm. They would park their small trailer where there was no electricity or water, but not too far from some small town where they could receive mail, haul water, and buy groceries.

They would spend their days either hiking or prospecting. The hiking helped to satisfy the wandering spirit they both possessed, and the prospecting was always a thrill. They expected each shovelful of dirt to contain the big nugget of gold they were looking for. Of

Mamma and Papa pause during their travels near Black Canyon City, Arizona, around 1948.

course they never became rich, but they always thought tomorrow would be the day they would become lucky. By living in a small trailer that could be pulled anywhere, no matter what the road conditions were, they were able to enjoy many different areas of our beautiful desert. I think that was the happiest time of their lives.

Papa passed away on the sixteenth of May, nineteen sixty-one, and we laid him to rest in the family plot in the Red Rock Cemetery.

Walter went to work for Coconino County, as he planned. That first summer after our return, he and Erma lived in their little tent at Mormon Lake where Walter was working. The following spring, in April, their first child Dorothy was born. Later they had three more children, Billy, Herbert, and another girl, Betty Jean. Erma and Walter lived the rest of their lives together in either Coconino or Yavapai counties. Walter passed away in nineteen sixty-one and Erma died on June twenty-first, nineteen seventy-five. They were both buried in the Red Rock Cemetery.

Virgie's husband, Burrell Russell, was working at the Clemenceau smelter when it shut down. Later he went to work at the State Rearing Ponds at Page Springs. He is now retired, but they still live in Yavapai County where they have spent all their married lives. They have three children, Lawton, Peggy and Wendell.

When I married my husband, Ray McBride, he was working in the Clemenceau smelter. We lived in one of the company houses where our daughter Gwendolyn was born. Ray worked at the smelter until the spring of nineteen thirty-seven, when the smelter shut down for the last time.

During the winter of nineteen thirty-seven and thirty-eight, we lived in a small cabin in Oak Creek Canyon on some property Papa had leased from the government. It was part of the flat where Manzanita Forest Camp is now. On March the third, nineteen thirty-eight, after a hard rain, Oak Creek came down in such a torrent that it washed my parents' chicken houses, their chickens, their barn and most of their orchard down the creek. Mamma and Papa were so discouraged they decided to sell their improvements and move away.

Ray and I were still living in the cabin on April the fifteenth when our son Ted was born. Papa had found someone to buy his improvements, but we didn't have to vacate the place until the first of July. Mamma and Papa were already in the process of moving to Lower Oak Creek, where they had rented a farm for the summer. Papa told us the cabin we were living in wouldn't be sold with the rest of his improvements, but we would have to find somewhere to move it. Ray had started work as an extra man on the highway to repair the road after that big flood, so we wanted to find somewhere in the Canyon to move the cabin. We received permission from Mamma's brother, Green Thompson, to move to the upper end of his property. We would be a short distance from the store on the west side of the creek and we could pay for the place by putting his badly-washed ditch back in working order, and furnish his wife with wood for the following winter.

The last week in June, I took the children and went to Williams to stay with Erma until Ray could tear our cabin down and move the lumber to its new location. We chose the only level spot on the place and put our cabin back together again. The rest of the ground was just one huge boulder pile; but after forty-odd years of work, we wouldn't trade this place for anywhere else we have been.

Violet's husband, Bill Rupe, was working at the Clarkdale smelter at the time it shut down. They moved to Winslow where Bill went to work for the Santa Fe Railroad. They had two children, Bob and Glenellen. When Bill retired they bought a place in Cornville where they were living when Violet died, on January nine-

The McBride home, after extensive remodeling and additions, as it looks today near Indian Gardens Terrace on Oak Creek. Cabin was originally located at Manzanita Forest Camp and brought to present site piece by piece after the spring flood of 1938.

teenth, nineteen seventy-five. She was buried in Red Rock. Their daughter lives in California and their son in Alaska, but Bill continues to live in Cornville. He spends most of this time hunting and fishing. The last two summers he has gone to Alaska where his son lives; and there he has caught many salmon and other fish that aren't in Arizona.

Bud (Albert Jr.) married Minnie Hanson when he was stationed in Kansas during his service in the army. They moved to Arizona when his enlistment was over, lived for a short time in Flagstaff, then moved to Phoenix where they are still living. Their four children, Robert,

Larry, Alberta and Phillip are living near their parents.

Chuckles, or Charley as we later called him, was injured in a car accident just north of our place. He passed away in the old Mercy Hospital in Flagstaff on February twenty-second, nineteen forty-one. We were all shocked and grief-stricken when we laid him to rest in the family plot at Red Rock. He was the first one of our

Clara Ellen Thompson Purtymun — Mamma — showing off her birthday cake at her ninety-first birthday party, April 7, 1978.

gang to part from this earth, and he was so young it was hard for any of us to accept the fact he was really gone.

Zola, the youngest member of our family, married Pete Hernandez in nineteen forty-five. They lived in Phoenix where their three children, Karren, Charles and Judy, were born. Pete was killed in a car accident on March the nineteenth, nineteen seventy-three. He was buried in Phoenix. Zola has spent her time since Pete's death between northern Arizona, where she and Pete had a summer cabin, and Phoenix, where two of her children live.

Mamma, now ninety-three, has been living in the Pioneer Home in Prescott for the past two years. She can still walk, but uses a walker most of the time. When the weather is nice in the winter and during the summer months, we bring her out to Oak Creek and she visits with her five living children, twenty-two grandchildren, forty-six great grandchildren, and twenty-three great great grandchildren.

Now as I look back on the trip we made so many years ago, I feel we all learned a lesson we never want to forget. Not one of us who made the trip has moved away from Arizona. After seeing a little of what the rest of the country looked like I think we learned to more fully appreciate our own state. We could have looked for years and never found a more beautiful and satisfying place to live than we have right here at home in our own state of Arizona.

Della and Kenneth Greenwell with their children, Virginia, Kay and Pat, around 1953.

Walter and Erma Baker, Billy, Dorothy (back), Betty Jean, and Herbert, about 1938.

The Russell family: Wendell Dee, Virgie, Lawton, Burrell and Peggy, taken around 1942.

The McBrides, Ray, Laura, Gwendolyn and Ted, 1953

Glenellen, Violet, Bill and Bobby Rupe around 1952.

Minnie and Albert (Bud) Purtymun, about 1953, and children Robert, Alberta and Larry.

Charles, Kaaron, Judy, Zola and Pete Hernandez, about 1953.

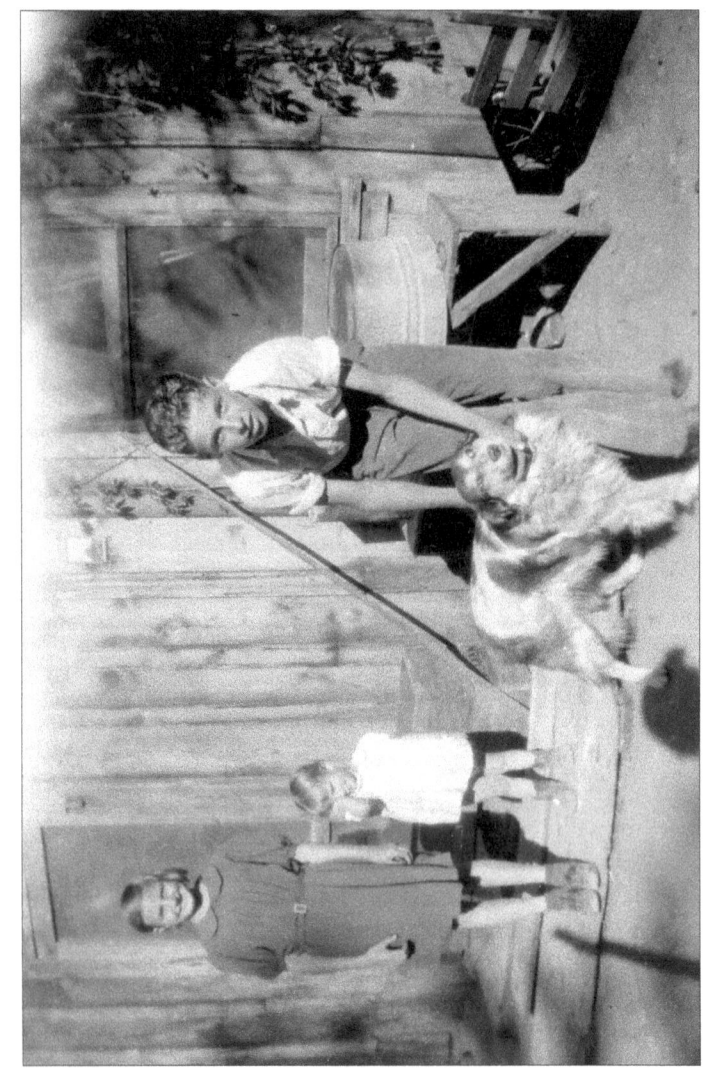

Zola, Gwendolyn and Charley P. (age 13 or 14) with his dog Bingo.

Mamma and Papa on their fiftieth anniversary in 1953.

www.ingramcontent.com/pod-product-compliance
Lightning Source LLC
Chambersburg PA
CBHW071419160426
43195CB00013B/1746